Brave by

-Faith-

STEPPING OUT IN FAITH AND DOING
WHAT GOD IS CALLING YOU TO DO

JULIETTE BUSH

Editors: Emily Juhnke and Grace & Co. Editorial Services (Dominique Bozeman)
Cover photo shot in Cape Town, South Africa by Justin Govender at inlitestudio.com
Cover Graphic Design: Norbert Elnar at masterpiecemovement.com
Chapter graphics designed by Freepik

*A special thanks and credit to contributing writers: Heather Lindsey, Cornelius Lindsey, Jon Norman, Romayne Jay, Norbert Elnar, and Cierra Cotton.

TABLE OF CONTENTS

Foreword 7

Dedication 10

Give honor when honor is due… 12

Introduction 15

Chapter 1: My Faith Journey 19

    Faith in Loss 22

    The Journey Continues 25

    Life of a Flight Attendant 29

Chapter 2: Step Out in Faith 33

    The Call 36

Chapter 3: Common Questions 45

    How do I know my purpose? 46

    How do I know God will provide? 48

    How do I know I will succeed and not fail? 51

    What if no one agrees? 54

    What if I feel like I'm not good enough? 56

    Fight back! 60

Chapter 4: No Money, No Problems: Life as a Missionary 63

Chapter 5: Spiritual Anorexia 75

Chapter 6: Faith in the Single Season 82

Chapter 7: Faith in the Transition into the Unknown 88

    God loves to spoil and surprise you: 94

    God provides at 40,000 feet: 95

Chapter 8: Letters: You've Got Mail 97

    The Great Unknown: From Cape Town, to the UK 99

    Leaving Corporate: From Australia to Cape Town 102

The Great Unknown: From State to State 106

Creative Design to God's Design................................. 109

Faith in Action: From Comfort to the Unknown 112

Chapter 9: Write, Baby, Write.. 115

Chapter 10: Don't Quit 124

Resource Guide.. 131

Encouraging Tools 144

Music... 146

Churches 147

Books.. 148

DVDs 149

If you have found yourself reading this book, I want you to know that you are in good hands. I have known Juliette for about a decade now, and I must say, this girl truly walks out what she preaches. She has been a true faith walker since the day I met her. I am so thankful that she has taken the time to put her journey in a book. She is the definition of being BRAVE BY FAITH.

I have watched her walk by faith, give by faith, serve the Lord by faith, and not hold tightly to what this world offers her. She gives what the Lord puts in her hands, and I truly believe that the Lord has given her a gift of giving. She not only gives of her time, energy, and money, but she also does it with a good attitude. I stand behind Juliette Bush in every word that she has spoken in this book. She is not here to boast or to make herself look good; but instead she is here to show you that you, too, can walk by faith in every single way.

I pray that as you read this book, you begin to truly walk by faith in every single area of your life and know that God will provide and take care of you. It may not look like you expected, but God will never, ever fail you. Remember that God doesn't send us out to walk by faith in things that are over our heads. Instead, this journey and process is from faith to faith and glory to glory.

I pray that the Holy Spirit opens up your heart as you read this book and that you walk by faith in every single way. I pray that you don't quit on the Lord and that you rest in Him.

"For unto whomsoever much is given, of him shall be much required: and to whom men have committed much, of him they will ask the more." - Luke 12:48 (KJV)

Remember that when you step out on faith with a pure heart, even if you feel like you missed God, He will find you.

Keep pressing forward. God loves you like crazy.

Love,
Heather Lindsey
heatherllindsey.com

This book is dedicated to **you**, the reader. I had no one in mind but you as I was writing this book. I believe that it is not by coincidence that you have it in your hands. I am praying for you on your journey.

Jesus Christ: Where do I even start? There are no words that can express the deep gratitude that I have toward you. You have shown me, yet again, that there is nothing impossible for you. You have put the desire of your heart in me to fulfill this book. Thank you for being the author of my life. I wouldn't change a thing.

My Mother, Laurie Collins: Mommy, thank you for being my first example of unconditional love. I believe God appointed you to be my mom in order for me to accomplish His will for my life. You have been there for me since day one of this faith journey and continue to be by my side. To that, I am grateful. To my entire family, thank you for your love and support!

Heather and Cornelius Lindsey: You two have been an integral part of my faith journey as mentors and friends. Thank you for pushing me closer to Christ. Your support and sharpening mean the world to me, and I truly am thankful for you two being there for me since the very beginning. I'm honored to do life and be on this journey together.

Stefan and Marcy Van der Male: Thank you for encouraging me, stretching me, and caring about me both individually as a person and through work-related projects. You two are on another level when it comes to leadership, character, and wisdom. Thank you, as well as the entire team at Hillsong Cape Town, for helping me to develop into my God-given potential.

Norbert Elnar: You have an incredible gift and call on your life. You work unto the Lord, and I am extremely blessed by you. Thank you for the book cover, graphic design work, logo for my blog, t-shirt designs, and more. I could go on. You always go above and beyond, and you are so patient! Thank you for your faithful service in this ministry and for being a great friend.

Dominique Bozeman: You have challenged me in this book, and I am grateful for your support. It was truly a divine appointment for you to be one of my editors. You are spirit-led in everything you do, and I am excited to see your gift continue to impact so many more people.

Emily Juhnke: Thank you for coming along this journey with me and for editing my book with such grace and love. Thank you for your accountability and prayers. You were so key in shaping this book. You are gifted, my friend, and I can't wait to see all of the amazing things God has in store for you.

Karolyne Roberts: Thank you for formatting my book. I truly appreciate you. You have been there for me since my very first blog. Wow! Thank you for being a wonderful friend. I love you more than words can say.

Thank you to **everyone** who has encouraged me and been there for me along this faith journey. There are too many of you to count, and I love and **value** each one of you.

Introduction

What does faith mean to you? If someone were to say, "Step out in faith," or "I trust by faith that God will see me through," would it just seem like gibberish? Would you know how to apply those statements to your life?

While growing up, you may have thought of faith as an opportunity to receive "blessings," such as a nice house, the newest car, or a better job. Maybe you experienced someone telling you to have faith, but you didn't know what you had to possess in order to see that through. Or maybe you heard the story of Noah's Ark as a child, but you never understood the full scope of what was demanded of Noah as a believer. As instructed, Noah built an ark after God warned him about a flood that would wipe out all of creation. Without seeing a single cloud in the sky, Noah followed through on God's commands. He had *faith* in what God told him. There are many examples and stories of faith in the Bible, but the true definition of faith is:

"... The confidence in what we hope for and assurance about what we do not see." – Hebrews 11:1

As Christians, we have full confidence in things that are not seen but that are *known* by faith in our hearts. My pastor uses this example: Imagine you're in a crowded room and hear your mom calling you. You can't see her, but you *know* it's your mom because you have spent time with her and recognize her voice. Hearing her is just as valid as seeing her.

The same applies to our faith in God. We can't physically see Him, but we can find assurance in Him through his Word and the ways He speaks to each of us individually.

"... Blessed are those who have not seen and yet have believed." – John 20:29

It can be so easy for us to rationalize things. However, the Word states that without faith it is impossible to please God (Hebrews 11:6). **This world encourages us to walk by reason and not by faith.** *But it's when we truly pick up our cross and follow Him that we will be living in true peace and abundance for our life.*

I want to share my faith journey with you. My goals in writing this book are to help you dive deeper into your relationship with God, encourage you to step out in faith, and provide you with resources to help you along in your journey.

I believe that it is no mistake that you have this book in your hands right now. Whether it was gifted to you or you bought it on your own, I believe God ordered your steps to encounter it. Maybe you're already confidently walking in God's purpose for this season of your life. Maybe you feel God calling you to make a change, but you're scared and anxious about what it would take. Maybe you have a desire to serve God, but are currently feeling a bit lost and directionless. Maybe the concept of stepping out in faith is completely new to you. Maybe you realize you've had a limited view of God and want to learn more about who He is and how He works. Maybe your relationship with God is just beginning.

Wherever you are in your walk with God, I pray that the stories and testimonies in the pages that follow will inspire and strengthen you to chase after God's amazing, ordained plans for your life!

Chapter 1:

MY FAITH JOURNEY

I was born on Christmas Day, 1985, in Queens, New York. I wasn't raised by my birth mom, as she couldn't take care of me, but that was okay because God still protected me and provided a mother for me. When I was 1, my father married my stepmom. She's the mother who raised me, and she has been an integral part of my faith journey to this day. She was my very first example of unconditional love, as she has always treated me as her own, even when she gave birth to my sister Jacquee two years after marrying my dad.

Growing up, we lived in Atlanta, Georgia, where my parents would take me and my sister to church every Sunday. Although we went to church each week, I didn't know God for myself. I would listen to what the pastor had to say, but I didn't read the Bible on my own. Essentially, I called myself Christian because my parents were Christians. I didn't have an intimate relationship with God for myself. My time with Him was limited to saying memorized prayers at dinner and before bed. I didn't know how to honestly pray to God or have a conversation with Him.

Despite all of that, I still felt that God was pursuing me and that He had a special covering and protection over my life. I felt His presence. I couldn't articulate it, but I knew in my heart He was always there with me. I knew God was calling me for something in His name. I knew He had a plan and purpose for me, but I didn't know what. I wasn't sure how to dig deeper into figuring that out.

He began to pursue me through other people. For example, when I was in middle school, I would be at the mall and someone I didn't know would come up to me, start a conversation, and invite me to their church. These kinds of moments would happen to me often. People were pursing me with the intention of bringing me closer to Christ. My mom encouraged me in this, but there also were others that would make fun of me. Often, to be cool and fit in, I would back away and make an excuse as to why I couldn't hang out or go to church with the person who had invited me. Still, God pursued me.

The bullying I experienced in this area of my life, and later on in others, caused me to become insecure in myself and in God. I felt like I wasn't enough. However, God turns around everything for our good. Situations where the enemy strategizes for harm, God is always there realigning things for our best.

Do not underestimate what God can do in the seasons where you don't know what to do.

Faith in Loss

One of the best and most important things that happened to me in my walk with God is the passing of my father. I know that sounds crazy, and you might be wondering why I would say something like that, but I didn't see my father's passing as losing him. I saw it as gaining a new kind of love — a love God demonstrates to us by being present without being seen; a love that is more real than any tangible object or earthly relationship. My father's passing led me to a renewed trust and faith in God as my Heavenly Father.

When I was 17, my father was diagnosed with chronic leukemia. Tumors, sickness, and death were always lurking around the corner, but he never showed it. No one even knew he had cancer unless they saw the tumors alongside his face. God was with him. He had more energy and focus than some of the healthiest people I knew. He didn't focus on the cancer. He focused on *life*. He had a peace that truly surpassed all understanding.

My father's cancer went into remission at one point, but it was on and off from then on. When I left for college, everything was going well with my father's health. That continued until I was a senior, but during the fall semester of that year, things started to get really bad. At 11 p.m. on April 27, 2008, one week before my college graduation, I received a phone call from my sister telling me that our father passed away.

When I first heard those words, it didn't even resonate with me. There was so much peace and calmness that I couldn't understand — it was seriously *supernatural*. I felt so much comfort. I went into my kitchen, and a few moments later, I had my first outer-body experience. I could see angels surrounding me, hugging me. I knew from that point on, Jesus was with me. My cares were His cares. **It was my first time experiencing the peace that truly surpasses all understanding.**

Just as the Holy Spirit is with us and we feel His presence, that is how I feel the presence of my father. To this day, He is alive in spirit and in my heart. While he was on earth, my father was a temporary guardian preparing me to take flight in the world. He taught me everything I needed to know in the flesh to prepare me for what I was supposed to accomplish through the spirit. **He protected me until I learned to turn to God for my protection.** Every life has a purpose. For my father, his purpose in my life was to mold, direct, and guide me into developing my own personal relationship with Jesus. This made it easier to submit to God.

Regardless of whether you do or do not have a father, lost a parent in your youth, were adopted, or feel abandoned, I encourage you to look to your Heavenly Father to fill the gap when you lose a loved one. As it says in Psalm 27:10, *"even if our father and mother abandon us, the Lord will receive us."* Be comforted in the fact that God has a purpose in everything, even if we don't understand at the present moment.

Love people while you are here, no matter what challenges they may face. Allow them to see the love of God through *you*.

In my father's passing, a blessing was discovered. Although I lost my earthy father, I gained a heavenly one. **Before I was his, I was the Lord's.**

The Journey Continues

After graduation and my father's passing, I moved back to Atlanta where it seemed like everyone was asking me what I was going to do next. Initially, I planned to work for my father, but since he passed, that plan was no longer a possibility. Although I didn't have a next step, I had peace in the midst of everyone pressuring me and asking questions. I didn't have a "plan B," but I knew God had a plan for me. I rested in that. It was hard to articulate this peace to others because it couldn't be fully explained in words.

My job search began. I graduated with a degree in marketing so, logically, the next step would be a corporate office job, right? I went to interview after interview, but nothing came of it. I even knew the CEO at one of the places I applied to, but I still didn't get the job. At the time, I was confused and discouraged, but I soon realized that what is not for you is simply not for you. It doesn't matter who you know. God will not open a door for you if it's not the right one.

A retail job was presented to me, and I decided to take it. Somehow, I knew I wouldn't stay there for long. After working in that job for a few months, God was pressing on my heart to move to New York right away. This was new to me because, although I had visited New York before, I had never considered living there. I resigned from my job, but I didn't plan to move to New York until two weeks later. During the time that I was delaying the move, my car was broken into twice, which set me back $1,500. I took this as a sign that I needed to stop dragging my feet and board that plane to New York immediately!

After arriving in New York, I realized the Lord was leading me to live and spend time with my birth mother. I stayed with her for almost a year and a half, which was a very difficult and challenging time in my life. Her path was very different from mine, and although I was still maturing in my walk with God, there was a lot of spiritual warfare whenever I was in her presence. Even in my struggle, God used that period tremendously, and I had favor wherever I went.

Within the first few weeks of being in New York, I received a job just across the street from where we were living. Later, a friend called to check in on me and talk to me about interviewing for a flight attendant job with a prominent international airline, Emirates, based in Dubai. She had just applied, and she thought that the job would be perfect for me as well. After looking into it, I immediately had peace about applying. The interview would take place right around the corner from where I lived at the time. While I wasn't sure how to prepare for an interview for a job like this, God gave me the words to say.

The interview had three rounds, and I was hired at the end of December. I was so excited, and I shared the news with everyone. Just four weeks before I was to leave, I received an email from the company saying that they had to put a hold on the offer because they had a freeze on all of the jobs. Due to the state of the economy at the time, they didn't know when or if they would renew the offer. Again, people were asking me, "So, what are you going to do?"

Even though the future of the airline was unclear, God gave me peace about it. He told me that I would be getting closer to Him that year, but I didn't understand this. I mean, I was already a Christian and went to church every week. What more could he want from me?

A couple months later, I came to know and interact with more of the young adults at the church I was attending and was truly astonished by what I experienced. These were all young, fly, Christian people, and it was my first time hearing anyone use God in their regular conversations like He was part of their daily life. I connected with everyone. They were all walking Bibles, and they did things in such a pure and fun way. These godly friendships really helped to shape my walk and were instrumental as I was developing my relationship with Christ.

Little did I know, God used the delay in my move to Dubai for me to develop godly friendships that would prune me and become life-long relationships. In August, I received an email that the airline would be in NYC and wanted to meet with me again. It wasn't a job offer, but they wanted to reconnect and see how I was doing.

During the months leading up to that phone call, the retail job I was working had become so monotonous. I had been actively looking for other opportunities and had received some callbacks for interviews. The first interview I went to didn't result in a job offer. While I was sitting in the reception area waiting to be called at another interview, the Lord told me to leave. He told me that I was wasting my time because I would be getting the airline job soon. More time went by, so I decided to take another interview. As I was walking there, the Lord told me to turn around and go back home — that I was wasting my time and that I should just trust Him.

When I was about to turn around, I received a call from Emirates giving me my new joining date. They said that I would be departing in just a few weeks! Really Lord?! God was truly so faithful to me during this period of waiting.

On December 1, 2009, a full year after my initial offer, I left the United States for Dubai. Out of the 96,000 people that applied for that position, I was one of 1,600 that were accepted. Although I didn't realize it at the time, God had a plan for me there that was greater than I thought and that was so much more than being a flight attendant.

Life of a Flight Attendant

When I first arrived in Dubai, it wasn't love at first sight. There was a lot of construction, as the country was still developing. It wasn't until I started training and making friends that my love for Dubai began to grow. As each day went by, I couldn't believe where I actually was. The position God gave me was one I never could have imagined. Being a flight attendant with such a prestigious airline was truly a dream job. The company provided us with everything. We had a furnished apartment, I didn't have to pay rent or bills, and I was dropped off and picked up from work each day. All I had to do was bring my luggage.

Each week, we flew to a different country on a double-decker plane — the largest in the world. Yes, you read that right, the largest in the world! I worked in premium class, and I was truly graced to do this job. God gave me favor in this, too, because it is where He wanted me to be.

I had several friends who applied for the job because they were attracted to the lifestyle and the glamour that came with it. They received the job and then quit after six months because it was too challenging. Just because a job seems physically appealing to us doesn't mean we are called to be there. I was graced to be in that position because God called me to be there. There are certain things that I am graced to do. If God is calling you to do it, you will be graced to do it. What He has called you to do, I won't necessarily be graced to do.

Traveling the world opened my eyes to see things from a different perspective. I was far away from home and living in a Muslim country, but God used my experiences there to draw me closer to Him. There were Christian churches in Dubai, but not one that I could resonate with or call home. I missed the fellowship and community of a church family. Around the time I was feeling this way, my friend and her husband started an online tele-church, The Gathering Oasis Church, as the beginning stages of their ministry. I had met them while living in New York City. They had sermons each Sunday and Tuesday over the telephone. I began listening to their messages, and this prompted me to start reading the Bible. I didn't draw closer to God by listening to their words, but by studying the Bible and applying its Word to my life in every way. I realized that I had previously been relying on my friend's and family's interpretations of the Word instead of pursuing God for myself.

As I studied the Bible and became more in-tune with God and His Word, my desires began to change. Soon after, I went on a missions trip to Kenya and volunteered at an orphanage.

It was an incredible experience, and I found myself thinking that this was something I'd love to do with my life. Instead of using my vacation days to save up money to go to Italy or Spain, I would research communities in need. I connected with non-profit organizations, fundraised for them, visited their bases, and ministered to the children.

From there, God continued to develop that calling within me. I was soon given the opportunity to plan and go on a missions trip to Ethiopia with key team members of The Gathering Oasis. This reconfirmed my desire and calling to the mission field, and I began to pray for what that would look like and where God wanted me to go next. I learned that you have to be careful what you pray for because God answered my prayers in away that was above and beyond what I ever expected.

Maybe God has called you somewhere, but you don't like it right now. Give it time to grow on you. For me, the purpose behind where I was more important than the location itself. Focus on the "why" and not the "where."

Looking back, I now see that God had everything lined up already. If I hadn't moved to New York, I wouldn't have connected with Emirates. If I hadn't been denied of other jobs, then I wouldn't have taken my dream job with them. If the move from New York to Dubai hadn't been delayed, I wouldn't have met the friends that are still an integral part of my journey today. If I hadn't taken the flight attendant job, I wouldn't have drawn as close to God as I did during my time in Dubai. I also wouldn't have heard of the city He had next for me. God is working behind the scenes on your behalf. Your life is not a surprise to Him. Do not worry.

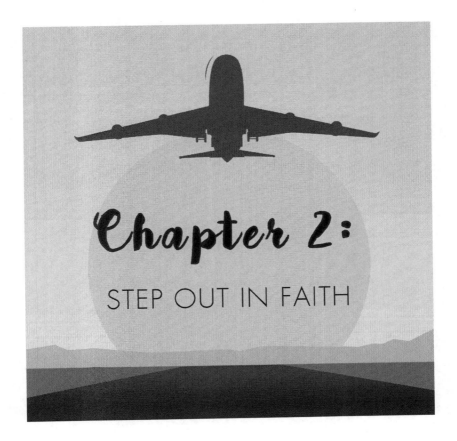

Chapter 2:

STEP OUT IN FAITH

"So don't worry about these things, saying, "What will we eat? What will we drink? What will we wear? These things dominate the thoughts of unbelievers, but your heavenly Father already knows all your needs. Seek the Kingdom of God above all else, and live righteously, and he will give you everything you need." – Matthew 7:31 (NLT)

When we step out in faith, we're fully trusting in God to carry us through a calling He's placed on our lives. During my second year living and working as a flight attendant in Dubai, the Lord told me to leave my job and move to Cape Town, South Africa, to do a one-year, unpaid community outreach internship at Hillsong Church.

I had been planning a holiday vacation to Cape Town, and I stumbled across the internship opportunity when researching for places to volunteer while there. Everywhere I go, I always look up Hillsong to see if they have a location where I'm traveling to because I love their worship. As I was on their website looking up possible opportunities to serve with their ministry in South Africa, I came across their "Year of Your Life" program. There were several different departments interns could be placed in, but the one that stuck out to me the most was their community outreach department, the Hillsong Africa Foundation, where you could serve and help build the community in Cape Town. *Was this real life?!*

It also was amazing to see that there were so many young people participating in the internship program. They weren't just locals, either. People from all around the world had left their comfort zones to follow God's will for their lives. Initially, the only other big example I had of what I desired to do was Mother Theresa, and she was so much older than me. I think society often associates this life with long skirts and old age, but these people were young and free in Christ and were fulfilling His call on their lives. Sign me up!

God really placed a conviction on my heart that I was meant to do this internship. He told me that He had *huge* plans for me there and that it would be an awesome testimony. I was excited about this calling because of my desire to do missionary work, but I didn't expect for it to happen so soon! I was worried about a lot of things.

The Call

"How will I survive? What will people think of me? I don't think I'm ready to leave my job yet, and I don't have enough money! I've never been to South Africa, and I don't know anyone there. What if I just wait one more year?"

All of these questions and thoughts were plaguing my mind after receiving the conviction to go to Cape Town. I had a nice apartment, a fabulous lifestyle, and a secure job. My job wasn't just any job — but a dream job! I soon realized that listening to God's prompting would require me to leave all of that behind.

I started to think, "Maybe it would be smart to stay at my current job for another year to save more money. Then when people ask me how I would afford and survive a year of volunteer work, I could have that as an answer."

I knew other people would be more comfortable with my decision if I had taken time to think it through and plan out my financial security. I wanted to make it seem as normal, practical, and sustainable as possible. I actually met up with a friend who was good at financial planning, and she put together a system to help me save money. So I told myself that I would stay in Dubai for one more year until I was financially secure enough to leave. I tried to rationalize with God, even though He clearly told me He had a huge purpose for me in Cape Town and that He would provide.

Has anything like that happened to you before? Have you ever felt God tell you to do something, but you second guessed His promises and delayed your obedience? Maybe you are in the middle of a decision like that at this very moment, deciding whether to obey God or to wait.

That year, I stayed in Dubai out of fear — fear of financial insecurity and fear of what others were going to think of me for making a sudden move and change in career. It honestly was the worst decision and time of my life. I chose to stay paralyzed in fear and insecurity instead of stand strong in God's promises and will for my life.

I had previously loved my job as a flight attendant so much because I was supposed to be there. I'd had favor and grace because I was walking in God's plans. But the year I told God "no," the covering was lifted. The favor with management, flights, and customers vanished. Each time I went to work, it truly felt like work. Even though I planned to save money, I actually had less money at the end of the year than when He first told me to go to Cape Town.

It was a very difficult time, but everything that happened also helped to deepen my relationship and trust in Him. I wasn't mad at God for everything I went through. I was upset that I let the fear of man replace the fear that I had in God. I realized that I had been placing fear of the opinions of others above my trust and faith in Him. God broke me of my bondage of other people's opinions, and I began to weigh His voice more heavily than the many conflicting voices of those around me.

"I tell you, my friends, do not be afraid of those who kill the body and after that can do no more. But I will show you whom you should fear: Fear him who, after your body has been killed, has authority to throw you into hell. Yes, I tell you, fear Him."
- Luke 12:4-6

As this inner transformation began to happen, my heart and spirit became ready to make the move to Cape Town. I became so confident in God's calling for the next season of my life. Staying in Dubai no longer appealed to me, and I no longer cared what others thought. I was fired up and expectant for what was to come, and no one could stop me.

Looking back, I can say that I'm happy and thankful for the challenges I faced during that year. If everything had gone smoothly, I likely would have delayed going to Cape Town again. It could have turned into a continuous cycle of running around and avoiding that step of faith.

We must stop allowing the voice of Satan to override the voice of God. We must start listening to and trusting God's plan and will for our lives.

What is God telling you to do? What has He put in your heart that you have delayed because of fear? Is it moving to an unknown land? Or maybe you have already stepped out in faith, but you are trying to finish everything in your own hands?

"Are you so foolish? After beginning by means of the spirit, are you now trying to finish by means of the flesh?" - Galatians 3:3

It can be so easy for us to start what God is telling us, only to finish it in the flesh. When we are saved, the Spirit of God lives inside of us. However, our sinful man, also called our flesh, wars against the spirit and desires to do what is contrary to what God wants us to do. This is when we pick up unnecessary burdens, stress, and more. If you have done this, don't think that you're the only one. It's something I constantly have to work on. At times, I've tried to blame it on the enemy before realizing that it's just a result of my disobedience and being out of His will for my life.

While I was in the season of making my decision to go from Dubai to Cape Town, South Africa, these were some of the scriptures that I held on to and that encouraged me:

> "Have I not commanded you? Be strong and courageous. Do not be afraid; do not be discouraged, for the LORD your God will be with you wherever you go." – Joshua 1:9

This encouraged me when I wanted to overthink things and be afraid of the unknown. The Lord has commanded us to be strong and not fear. That means we have an option to rest in His peace or in the fear of others. This is a daily choice that we have to intentionally be aware of and do. We will be afraid, as it is a natural emotion, but the Lord wants to reassure us that He will be there. We do not have to fear because He will be there with us — whether it be a new job where you don't know a soul, a new country where you are getting settled in, or in transition trusting Him for the next direction. Listen to the Holy Spirit. He is the best leader, and He will not fail us.

> "'For my thoughts are not your thoughts, neither are your ways my ways,'' declares the LORD." – Isaiah 55:8

I meditated over this when I didn't understand the path that God was instructing me to take. We have to understand this important scripture and confide in it, as many things God tells us to do won't make sense to our carnal nature. If someone isn't a believer, it sure won't make sense to them. This scripture helped to mold my thought pattern. It enabled me to move forward and put into play what the Holy Spirit was prompting me to do. Do not limit Him to your own understanding. ✝ ✝ ✳

"Trust in the Lord with all your heart and lean not on your own understanding." – Proverbs 3:5

I confided in this scripture when I didn't know how I was going to live without any financial security. We have to trust in the Lord. Our flesh wants to trust in the things we can see — like our savings plan, for example. The Lord says, *"Blessed are the pure in heart, for they will see God"* (Matthew 5:8). Your heart is so important and significant in this. You have to be all in. Your heart can't waver or be lukewarm. Sometimes we won't understand why things roll out the way they do, but the fruit of your obedience will come through doing what God is telling you to do.

"But whoever disowns me before others, I will disown before my Father in heaven. Do not suppose that I have come to bring peace to the earth. I did not come to bring peace, but a sword. For I have come to turn a man against his father, a daughter against her mother, a daughter-in-law against her mother-in-law — a man's enemies will be the members of his own household." – Matthew 10:33-36

This scripture helped me when I began to worry about what others would say or think. We can't deny God or be embarrassed and ashamed of what He has called us to do. Not everyone is going to understand it, but that's okay. It's your calling, not theirs. If the enemy can't get to you, then he will go through your family or friends to try and stop you or stall you. We see an example of this in Genesis where the enemy couldn't get through to Adam to eat the apple, so he went through his wife Eve. If people around you are tempting you to quit, hold on to God's voice and remember the passage above. When He calls you to His kingdom, He will separate you from anything that deviates from that. That includes those who are close to you if they are drawing you away from what God is telling you to do. The Bible does say to honor your parents, but if their lives and their wisdom don't honor or glorify God, then this doesn't apply.

God will not ask you to do something if He doesn't have a plan to see it through. He won't put a desire in your heart that He doesn't have His hand over. If it's His will, it's His bill. This, however, doesn't mean that it will always be easy. Trials and tribulations are promised in the Bible, but He tells us not to fear and to have peace (John 16:33).

I encountered many roadblocks on my journey. Many of which prepared me for seasons that came later on. God is constantly preparing, pruning, delivering, and healing us, even when we don't recognize it in the moment. When we do things God's way, He will be there for us. I have learned that as you move, God moves. As you take the first step, He will make sure there is a stone in place for your next.

Throw away your five-year plan, and make room for God to move in your life. It will be better than the one you could ever imagine, plan, or comprehend on your own.

Right before leaving for Cape Town, I actually received three job opportunities in Dubai. My dream before deciding on the internship would have been to fly for a private government airline, and God told me that I would receive an opportunity to do just that before departing for South Africa. I laughed at first but, sure enough, just three weeks before I departed I received a phone call regarding a position with a private airline. A few days later, I received another job opportunity to do business promotions for Emirates. Then another opportunity working as a personal assistant for a high profile person in Dubai came along soon after.

I had all of these opportunities, but none of them appealed to me. In fact, I cut the conversation short and said, "No, thank you," to the private airline job, as well as to the other two. I wasn't interested. I know I could have chosen to pursue one of those opportunities and God still would have loved me, but He had already called me somewhere else. He told me that He had a huge plan and purpose for me in Cape Town.

Following God's plans has literally blown my "dream" plans out of the water! Being denied of what I *thought* I wanted opened up His plan for my life to travel to over 36 countries, live on three continents, and experience such magnificent things such as walking a tiger in Thailand, gliding down the

Great Wall in China, learning the true meaning of "Ubuntu" in South Africa, riding an elephant in Bali, dancing at Carnival in Brazil, riding a gondola in Italy, and watching the sunset by the Eiffel Tower in the heart of France.

Living in our calling isn't boring, and we don't need connections to do amazing things. We just need to be connected to the One who is the source of everything.

I hope my journey will you encourage you to step out in faith and do what God has called you to do. Whatever that may be for you, trust Him for grace, strength, and provision. You will have true peace, joy, confidence, and comfort when you're exactly where you're supposed to be. If you haven't spent much time with God lately, I invite you to do that before continuing on in this book. Pull out the Bible. Take some time to talk to God and read His Word. Time spent with him is where you'll receive the revelation of His plans for you. Seek Him first, and then everything else will be added unto you.

Chapter 3:

COMMON QUESTIONS

How do I know my purpose?

The inventor of an object is generally the best source of information on how that object works. You might be able to use the invention in many ways through coming up with your own ideas or asking others for theirs, but you likely wouldn't be using it to its fullest potential without seeking instructions from its creator first.

The same applies to how we are meant to use our lives. We often depend on our families, friends, teachers, mentors, and those around us for direction, instead of seeking the Holy Spirit. God created you. Before you were born, He set you apart. He knows you and your purpose better than anyone else (Jeremiah 1:5, Psalm 139:13).

How do you know your purpose from God? By spending time with Him through praying, seeking His voice, and reading His Word. This is something you have to do intentionally on a daily basis. Romans 12:12 encourages us in this: *"Be joyful in hope, patient in affliction, faithful in prayer."* As you continue to spend time with Him, you will become more aware of the ways He speaks to you. He will reveal things to you at the right time you need them, and your seasons will line up accordingly.

He is always busy developing and preparing you for what is coming next.

We each have unique gifts given to us by God, and He uses these gifts to equip us for our purposes. We can't carry out our life purposes on our own. We need God. For when we are weak, He is strong. Resist the urge to meticulously plan out every detail of your life. How is God supposed to come through for you when you are coming through for yourself?

I'm not saying to be lazy. It's good to have dreams and goals, but remember to make God's vision for your life your main priority. Leave room for your plans to intertwine with His. This involves dying to yourself in order for God's name to be glorified. Our life is for God's glory. When you surrender your life to God's and allow Him to paint your story, it will become a masterpiece. When you are living in your purpose, you will have peace. Your hope will be in God's words and promises. God will never fail you.

Everyone's purpose and destination is different, but it is all equal in bringing glory to God.

How do I know God will provide?

Once you become more in-tune with where God is leading you, you might start to wonder how He will provide for it. God's provision for you may look different than His provision for someone else. You could be relying on God for your next meal, while someone else could be trusting that He will provide their tuition next month. There have been months at a time where I wasn't sure where my food or rent would come from while volunteering, but God always provided. Whatever it is for you, the Lord does not want us to be anxious or worried. For He states in Matthew 6:25-34:

"Therefore I tell you, do not worry about your life, what you will eat or drink; or about your body, what you will wear. Is not life more than food, and the body more than clothes? Look at the birds of the air; they do not sow or reap or store away in barns, and yet your heavenly Father feeds them. Are you not much more valuable than they? Can any one of you by worrying add a single hour to your life? And why do you worry about

clothes? See how the flowers of the field grow. They do not labor nor do they spin. Yet I tell you that not even Solomon in all his splendor dressed was dressed like one of these. If that is how God clothes the grass of the field, which is here today and tomorrow is thrown into the fire, will He not much more clothe you—You of little faith? So do not worry, saying, 'What shall we eat?' or 'What shall we drink?' or 'What shall we wear?' For the pagans run after all these things, and your heavenly Father knows that you need them. But seek first his kingdom and his righteousness, and all these things will be given to you also. Therefore do not worry about tomorrow; for tomorrow will worry about itself. Each day has enough trouble of its own."

According to His Word, He is our provider. Be encouraged by Philippians 4:19, as it says, "And my God will meet all your needs according to the riches of His glory in Christ Jesus." **Where God leads, He will meet your needs.**

I've found that people have no problem believing that God created and formed them, but it is hard for them to believe that God will provide for them. Why is this? In the Western culture, we are rational thinkers. This can make it so easy for us to become our own "god." We think we don't need a Savior because we have our savings account or someone else we can rely on. We are more confident in our own "plan B" than the "plan A" that God initially created for us. The act of stepping out in faith sometimes only happens when things look "right" or when all of our ducks are in a row.

But that is not *faith*. When you do that, you are delaying your obedience. There is a reason God calls you to do something in a certain season. There are people waiting for you to fulfill your calling and step out in faith. Living in faith allows Jesus to really take control of your life.

It can be scary to step out in faith, especially when going somewhere or doing something completely new. At times, you might slip in the timing. The Lord knows that I have. I haven't always stepped out in faith right when He called me to. When that happens, God will continue to test us — not to punish us, but to strengthen our faith.

Wherever He sends you, there is a plan for you. Each season, good or bad, is a piece of the puzzle that forms your complete masterpiece. It might not make sense right now, but you will begin to see the pieces come together as you continue to trust and obey. God will provide for you. His Word is true, and He will not fail you.

How do I know I will succeed and not fail?

First, we must define success. Success means different things to many people. In this context, success is living in God's will for your life. You could be doing great work somewhere, but if God told you to do something else, you are not living in His will for your life. People are waiting for you to step out in faith. There is someone or some place you are meant to reach. They are waiting for you to fulfill God's ordained call on your life. Bottom line: Success is *living* and *resting* in what God calls you to do. MAJOR KEY

You may see someone who has it all, but does not live a life according to God's standards. **If you have to sin to get it, it's not a blessing.** Do not look to them and try to emulate what they are doing, for the Lord encourages us by saying:

"Do not fret because of those who are evil
or be envious of those who do wrong;

for like the grass they will soon wither,

like green plants they will soon die away.

Trust in the Lord and do good;

dwell in the land and enjoy safe pasture.

Take delight in the Lord,

and he will give you the desires of your heart.

Commit your way to the Lord;

trust in him and he will do this:

He will make your righteous reward shine like the dawn,

your vindication like the noonday sun.

Be still before the Lord

and wait patiently for him;

do not fret when people succeed in their ways,

when they carry out their wicked schemes.

Refrain from anger and turn from wrath;

do not fret—it leads only to evil.

For those who are evil will be destroyed,

but those who hope in the Lord will inherit the land.

A little while, and the wicked will be no more;

though you look for them, they will not be found.

But the meek will inherit the land

and enjoy peace and prosperity."

- Psalm 37:1 -11

The world might try to tell you that success means getting married, having a great job, or making a lot of money. Remember that you live for an audience of One. Your life path and success are determined by God's voice and Word, not by the biased opinions of others. When you are being led by the Holy Spirit, you will not fail. His Word is a lamp unto our feet and a light upon our paths (Psalm 119:105).

What if no one agrees?

The idea of pleasing people and being liked by everyone is a major problem of the world. We all want to be affirmed. We all want to be accepted by others, congratulated for our accomplishments, and acknowledged for a job well done. But when our desire for acceptance keeps us from stepping out in faith and doing what God calls us to do, it becomes very dangerous.

It is possible that many people in your life will not understand what God is calling you to do. They might give you advice based on what they would do in your situation. They might even have the best intentions and want the best for you. This can make it hard to follow through, but remember that He called you to do it — not them.

If the disagreements are coming from people who do not have a strong relationship with Christ and have not walked in faith or depended on God as their provider, they likely are not going to believe in His power to do so for you. That is okay. God might have placed you among those people for a reason

— to be a light and example that helps to draw them closer to Him. Your obedience will be a testimony to them and reveal God's glory.

Matthew 10:34-35 reminds us that we can't put our family's opinions above God's voice. You have to be focused on God and believe that He will take care of you, no matter what others think. At the end of the day, you answer to God — not them. Remember that Jesus himself was mocked and disrespected in his own hometown.

"If the world hates you, keep in mind that it hated me first. If you belonged to the world, it would love you as its own. As it is, you do not belong to the world, but I have chosen you out of the world. That is why the world hates you. Remember what I told you: 'A servant is not greater than his master.' If they persecuted me, they will persecute you also. If they obeyed my teaching, they will obey yours also. They will treat you this way because of my name, for they do not know the one who sent me. If I had not come and spoken to them, they would not be guilty of sin; but now they have no excuse for their sin. Whoever hates me hates my Father as well. If I had not done among them the works no one else did, they would not be guilty of sin. As it is, they have seen, and yet they have hated both me and my Father. But this is to fulfill what is written in their Law: 'They hated me without reason.'" - John 15:18-25

What if I feel like I'm not good enough?

If you struggle with feelings of inadequacy, you're not alone. This is something I'm constantly working to overcome. I even started to have those thoughts as I was writing this book. I began to look at myself as if I was not good enough. I began to second guess myself, and I wondered if I really had what it took.

When we allow our fears to keep us from accomplishing God's will for our lives, we become paralyzed. You may think of paralysis as a physical condition, but we can also become spiritually paralyzed — frozen in fear. When we listen to our doubts, we are allowing the enemy to take control of our hearts and minds. He knows our weaknesses, and he will try to take advantage of them. We can't continue to give him a foothold into our lives.

When God calls us to do something, he will equip us to carry it forward into completion — even when it seems like an impossible task. The story of Moses is a great example of this.

He stuttered and didn't think he could say God's word eloquently enough, but God called him to speak and lead a nation! Moses felt inadequate and insecure, and he didn't have the confidence to do it. He even pleaded with God to choose someone else:

"O Lord, I'm not very good with words. I never have been, and I'm not now, even though you have spoken to me. I get tongue-tied, and my words get tangled." - Exodus 4:10 (NLT)

Because of his stutter, Moses was worried that he couldn't do what God called him to do. He thought people wouldn't take him seriously. What are you feeling inadequate about? Do you feel that if you just had more of this or didn't have that, then you would be good enough for God's call? Whenever you feel this way, remember that God calls us in our weakness so *He* will be glorified.

In Exodus 4:11, the Lord told Moses, *"Who makes a person's mouth? Who decides whether people speak or do not speak, hear or do not hear, see or do not see? Is it not I, the* Lord*? Now go! I will be with you as you speak, and I will instruct you in what to say"* (NLT).

Moses pushed through. Even when he was afraid and didn't understand, he continued to do what God was calling him to do. I encourage you to do the same! God was able to accomplish incredible things through Moses because of his decision to trust and obey. He has big plans for you, too.

Another example is David and Goliath in 1 Samuel 17. David was a shepherd, the youngest of the eight sons of Jesse of Bethlehem. King Saul and his men were battling the Philistines, one of which was a 9-foot giant named Goliath. Goliath was challenging God's people to stand up to him and demonstrate that their God was more powerful than he was. The men of Saul's army were afraid of Goliath. There was no one willing to step out in faith and face the giant, until David came into the Israelite camp.

David protested that He could kill the giant, but Saul replied:

"Don't be ridiculous! There's no way you can fight this Philistine and possibly win! You're only a boy, and he's been a man of war since his youth" (NLT).

Maybe you're in a similar position right at this moment. You're fired up, but other people are putting you down to the point where you start to feel inadequate to answer God's call.

But David, filled with faith and passion for God's name, slew Goliath with a stone and a sling. He then cut off Goliath's head with the giant's own sword.

David's faith was so strong that he believed the Lord would go with him and enable him to defeat Goliath (1 Samuel 17:36-37). David's faith was born out of his experience with God's grace and mercy in his life up to that point. The Lord had delivered him out of dangerous situations in the past, proving His power and trustworthiness, and David relied on Him to deliver him from the Philistine.

From the story of David and Goliath, we can learn that the God we serve is capable of defeating any of the giants in our lives — fear, financial issues, doubts of faith — if we know Him and His nature well enough to step out in faith. When we do not know what the future holds, we have to trust Him. Knowing God through His Word will build our faith in Him.

He cares deeply for us. Sometimes that involves trials and battles, but these are ultimately for our good and His glory. James tells us to consider it pure joy when we encounter trials because they test our faith and develop patience and perseverance (James 1:2-4). When we are tested by these trials, we can, in the power of the Lord, stand up against any giant, trusting Him to win the victory as we step out in faith.

Fight back!

If you find yourself struggling with any of the thoughts and questions in this chapter, I encourage you to fight back!

"For our struggle is not against flesh and blood, but against the rulers, against the authorities, against the powers of this dark world and against the spiritual forces of evil in the heavenly realms." - Ephesians 6:12

There are spirits specifically assigned to stop you from fulfilling what God is calling you to do. They will try to take you down, but don't let them. Don't give up! Fight back with a burning passion and zeal to fulfill the plans that God has started within you.

Tell someone: The Bible tells us to confess our sins to one another and to pray for each other (James 5:16). Talk to someone that you can trust and confide in. Share with them what you are struggling with — don't be ashamed. They can help you see the bigger picture of God's calling and encourage you out of the rut you are in (Proverbs 27:17).

Talk to God: Most importantly, don't abandon your time with God. He is our healer and our leader. If you start to feel lost in your fears and doubts, go to Him. He is always there to get you back on track.

"For I know the plans I have for you," declares the LORD, *"plans to prosper you and not to harm you, plans to give you hope and a future." - Jeremiah 29:11*

"Have I not commanded you? Be strong and courageous. Do not be afraid; do not be discouraged, for the LORD *your God will be with you wherever you go." – Joshua 1:9*

"Now go; I will help you speak and will teach you what to say." – Exodus 4:12

Can I pray for you?

"Lord, thank you for the call that you have over this reader's life. Thank you for the assignment you have given them. I rebuke any demonic spirits or forces that are coming against their mind, thought, or physical being. Make them sensitive to the devil's scheme, which will give them more passion to do what you have called them to do. Even when they do not know what to say or do, give them the right words and actions

in this call. Help them to trust you, and know that they will not be defeated. Help them to be vulnerable to their friends. Give them discernment to share what they are going through so they can pray together. Thank you for your grace and your mercy over their life. In Jesus' name, Amen."

Chapter 4:

NO MONEY, NO PROBLEMS: LIFE AS A MISSIONARY

"Therefore go and make disciples of all nations, baptizing them in the name of the Father and of the Son and of the Holy Spirit." - Matthew 28:19

What comes to mind when you hear the word "missionary?" Do you think of the Bible times, or do you think of the present? What do you think missionaries do?

A missionary is someone who takes on the full-time task of sharing the message, love, generosity, and care of Jesus to the nations — in whatever way or place God leads them.

Currently, there are millions of missionaries all over the world. If God has called you to step out into the unknown to be a missionary, I pray the testimonies of God's faithfulness in my journey will inspire you to do just that. If God has placed a different calling on your life, I pray that the chapter that follows will further encourage you to fully embrace and step into that calling. He will use you, wherever He may lead.

As I mentioned previously, I first felt God calling me to serve Him through missions work when I was in Ethiopia on my second missions trip. At first, I had no idea that this would involve becoming a full-time missionary. **When we answer God's call and step out in faith, we don't always see every piece of the puzzle right away.** But now I can't see myself doing anything else. Missions work has become a lifestyle and passion of mine.

After my interview and acceptance into the internship program at Hillsong in Cape Town, South Africa, I was so anxious and excited to make the move. I couldn't wait another minute. I didn't tell a lot of people or make a huge announcement about it because I knew that people were going to try to shake my faith. I wasn't financially stable, and my decision to move probably wouldn't have made a lot of sense to some people.

However, I gave that burden to God, and He carried it for me. He held all of the details; I just had to move. I remember receiving so much confirmation during the year leading up to me leaving. I started meeting many people that told me they were from Cape Town — strangers, people on the streets, someone on a flight. Even my sister told me she met someone from Cape Town. It was unreal. I knew my time was coming soon.

In preparation for the move, I just packed my things. God specifically told me not to fundraise or ask anyone for money. Just as He put it on my heart to go, He would put it on other people's hearts to support me. **He wanted me to focus on my work. As I built His house, He would build mine.**

He gave me this analogy: Just as I go to my parent's house and know that I have a place to stay, food to eat, a bed to sleep in, and a pillow to lay my head on, it was the same with Him. Imagine what He would do for me, Him being my Heavenly Father.

I spent a lot of time praying about this, and God continuously confirmed it for me. This was not to be done in my own strength because it wasn't my own will — it was His.

I realize this might not have been the most popular or common way to go about something like this. As humans, we like to brainstorm and think about all of our options and plans. We like to know exactly how we are going to make something work, but if we give the situation to God and focus on Him, His plans will prevail.

Many obstacles and challenges were ahead of me in Cape Town. There was a lot I could have been worried about. Housing, food, transport, and flights were not included in the internship. So not only was I going to be working for free as a volunteer, but I also had to pay a good amount to move and live there. I had never been to Cape Town before, and I didn't know a single soul there. However, I wasn't worried one bit. I had peace that surpassed all understanding, and I knew that God was going to work everything out.

When you do volunteer work overseas, there is a lot of initial behind the scenes work you have to get done. One of the big things I had to do was apply for a visa, which permits you to stay in the country of your volunteer work for a certain period of time. This process requires you to submit many documents such as proof of finances, international health insurance, airfare confirmation, medical records, police clearance, and more. Every single one of these requirements has a fee, but I know plenty of people who God has provided for and who have gotten visas with items missing from their application. If God has a purpose for you to be somewhere and it's in His will, then He will make it happen. I'm not saying there won't be challenges, but don't lose hope in going after God's call. Obstacles give God the opportunity to fill in those gaps and perform miracles right in front of your eyes.

I can attest to God's goodness and faithfulness in this area. I was living in Dubai when I applied for my volunteer visa. The rule at the embassy was that you had to be a resident of the applying country or live there for at least five years in order to apply for a volunteer/study visa. Although I didn't fit those requirements, I still filled out my application and stood in line with hope and confidence that I was going to get my visa that day. To my surprise, they denied me. I wasn't disappointed, and my stomach didn't drop. I knew God would take care of it.

The teller at the embassy told me that even if my application were accepted, it would take at least three weeks for them to process it. I also would have to leave my passport at the embassy for the duration of the approval process. Being a flight attendant at the time required me to have my passport at all times because I flew to different countries each week. Without it, I would be out of work and money for however long it took to process my volunteer visa. On top of that, a full-fare ticket from Dubai to America to get my visa would be $1,500+. Still, I wasn't worried. I knew God would make a way.

Soon after I stepped out of the line, a man walked up to me who had been standing in line beside me. He said, "God bless you for the work you are doing. I heard your story, and I actually know the person who signs off for the visas. I can't promise you anything, but I can see what I can do. The guy is away on holiday but will be back in two weeks."

I gave him my details, and he phoned two weeks later telling me to bring my documents to the embassy. He introduced me to his friend who signs off for the visas, and I gave him my documents. Two days later, I went back to the embassy to collect my visa. It was approved and stamped in my passport. How good was God?!

The same man I met in the line personally took me to the police station and walked me through getting my police clearance. He knew everyone in there and spoke Arabic, so it was a quick and easy process. Without him, it would have taken a lot of time and stress to do. God sent an angel to help me through it all.

God also came through with all of my medicals. I wasn't even seeking help. God just sent His blessings to me. A person I spoke to in church told me they knew someone who works at the hospital and that they would see if he could get me a discount. I made my appointment through him, and he said that I could get 25 percent off, which was great. When I went to pay, the teller told me I was actually going to get 50 percent off. However, when I received the invoice, it totaled only 25 percent of the initial cost. I received 75 percent off for all my medicals! I didn't have much money at the time, so it was a huge blessing! It was like God telling me that He had it under control.

I didn't tell anyone or make a big deal out of the fact that I didn't have a lot of money. I was content knowing that everything was going to be taken care of. God will do the same for you. God can cancel debts, decrease costs, and send people your way to help you out, but you won't see the provision unless you step out in faith. It seemed impossible for me to apply and receive a visa in Dubai, as well as pay a decreased fare for my medicals. But God makes a way out of no way. The impossible, He makes possible. It wasn't until I stepped out in faith and moved forward in the process of applying that God made the provisions.

Accommodation for my stay Cape Town was another area that God provided for. After just one Google search, I found the accommodation that I stayed at during most of my duration there — a student hostel that houses 40 women. Even though I hadn't been officially accepted for the internship yet, I knew that was where the Lord purposed me to be. I emailed the hostel manager and wired money to pay a non-refundable deposit in order to hold my room there.

Some of my family members were confused as to why I paid my deposit to a place I knew so little about. One said, "They could be crazy people!" I would be sharing a room with another girl at the hostel. To that my sister said, "What if she steals?!" Well, what if we become the best of friends and encouragers of each other? What if God has a purpose for the relationship and divine connection of us staying with each other? No matter what people said, I had peace about it.

I prayed for my roommate and the girls before I moved to the hostel. I could have lived anywhere in Cape Town, but I lived at this hostel intentionally because God was calling me there to be a light. I had lived in nice houses and had been living in one of the best apartments in Dubai for the past three years of my life, but I was going to Cape Town for a mission. I was going not to be comfortable, but to do the Lord's work. In living outside of my comfort zone, I knew God would strengthen my peace and contentment in Him.

After a few months of living in the hostel, I wanted out. Comparison started to kick in because I would see other interns and volunteers who lived in beautiful apartments right across the street within walking distance of church. I started telling God I could serve Him better if I lived in a more comfortable and modern place near church. I soon had the opportunity to move into one of the most sought out apartments in that area. However, I quickly noticed that the grass is not always greener on the other side.

Before even moving in, I had a feeling it wouldn't work out. But I was desperate to move, and thought it was a "God hook-up" because the door was open. I realized that **every open door does not lead us to the things of God.** I should have prayed and sought God before I made the decision, but I didn't because I wanted to rush it.

I wasn't graced to be there. My funds ran low, and I actually was spending more money living there than I had been in the hostel. There was a mall that was walking distance from my apartment, and it had so many shops and restaurants with yummy food. The thought that I would save money by moving closer to church was far from the truth because it actually opened the gate for me to indulge even more. I also could see the grace and favor in my internship diminishing. My mind was all over the place, and I also lived with a very challenging roommate.

After three months of living there, I wanted to move. I looked up availabilities through an online portal, but nothing seemed to work out. I phoned my old accommodation, knowing that the only way I could move back was if my previous room was still available. I didn't want any other space. Sure enough, it was available. The girl that was sharing with my old roommate had just moved out because she no longer could afford it. It was like God saying He forgave me for stepping outside His will. He was welcoming me back with open arms. It was truly a miracle. All of the other rooms were full. God had opened the door for me to move back in.

Looking back, I can see how God was able to use that challenging season of my life for good. Having a difficult roommate caused me to grow and develop as a person. Living so much closer to church enabled me to flourish in relationships. I led a Connect group and was able to build friendships that continue to be influential in my life.

When I moved back into the hostel, the things that bothered me previously didn't bother me anymore. One reason I had moved out was because there was no air conditioning. I would sweat in my sleep, and I was miserable. When I left, I realized that no apartment had air conditioning — even the best! I actually wasn't missing out. I was overthinking everything, and the "better" apartment was just an illusion. Moving back also ignited my fire to move in my calling and purpose. I had more grace in my behaviors and interactions with others.

Many people thought our accommodation, transport, and other costs were included in volunteering. However, when I say that we worked for free, we worked for free! We found our own apartments, and we had rent and bills just like any other average person, but God still came through and *provided!*

People would visit and give me money, from strangers to family to friends. The people I *thought* would support me, *didn't,* and the people who I never thought would, *did.* I'm happy it worked out that way because it showed me God's faithfulness.

As volunteers, our job description wasn't just to do menial tasks. It was a real, full-time job. We worked from 9-5/exempt, meaning we left when the work got done — based on our own conviction. Our tasks involved leading teams, pioneering initiatives, managing projects, mentoring, and so much more. We were entrusted with a lot, and we were seen as leaders from day one.

When you work for a salary, you get what you get, and that's it. When you work for the Lord, there isn't a cap. He supersedes your needs, your wants, and even your desires. He is your provider.

It surprised me because I knew people with salaries who would complain how they didn't have enough money for *this* or were living paycheck to paycheck to pay *that*. I found myself thinking, "Man, the faith life seems to have more security than working. Shouldn't we be the ones complaining?" **But when you are exactly where you are supposed to be, doing what God has called you to do, you will have everything you need.**

Still, I can relate to their feelings. When I had a salary, I would get stressed out if I didn't have enough money at the end of the month because I was doing it in my own strength. I have so much peace now, even when I have little, because I know God cares for me. As I work unto the Lord, He sees all things.

Although the internship stretched me, it was the most amazing season of my life. One of the projects I was a part of at the Hillsong Africa Foundation was creating an early childhood development curriculum for moms with babies. Being a part of this team and going to the communities each week filled my heart with so much love and joy.

One thing that made this program different from any other job or program I've been a part of was that they cared about how you grew as a person. It didn't matter if your project was going perfectly or whether or not you had the best ideas.

Success was measured in how you were developing as a person — spiritually, personally, and more.

Another part that I will always cherish are the friendships I made. Although we were all from different parts of the world, we had all heard God call us to move there. I thought it was amazing that I stepped out in faith to do one year. But when I started to meet people that were in their 2nd, 3rd, 4th, or 5th year of *living by faith*, it blew my mind! Seeing this really encouraged me. I knew if God provided for them, He could do it for me too.

Someone, somewhere is waiting for your obedience to step out in faith. You see, your obedience is not just about you. It's about the people you encounter and others you may not even know you are tied to. When I moved to Cape Town and started blogging about it, it led six other people I didn't know across four different continents to do this internship, as well as dozens of others who have stepped out in faith to leave their home to the unknown. My blog was a stepping-stone and bridge to do what they are doing now. There are people waiting for you to step out in faith and do what God is calling you to do.

I volunteered in Cape Town for three years, but living by faith is not just for a season, a mission trip, or a day. It's a lifestyle. It's a journey. There is no formula to it, and it will look different for everyone, but He is equally faithful to all of us and to the specifics in what He has called us to do.

Chapter 5:

SPIRITUAL ANOREXIA

According to the National Eating Disorders Association, Anorexia Nervosa is, "A serious, potentially life-threatening eating disorder characterized by self-starvation and excessive weight loss." As Christians, our spiritual food is the Bible, or the Bread of Life. When you deprive your spirit of the Word, you are starving it of important nutrients it needs to grow and thrive to its fullest potential. You are keeping your spirit from producing the fruits of love, joy, peace, forbearance, kindness, faithfulness, gentleness, and self-control (Galatians 5:22-23). This is spiritual anorexia.

No one is exempt from this. We are all humans, and we all have struggles during our walk with God. I've been there before, and I've especially found that it's easy to fall into spiritual anorexia when serving in full-time ministry. When you're serving, your days are often filled with reading the Bible, studying for sermons, and praying for others. This can be spiritually draining to the point that when you go home at night, you might just want time to rest. The thought of picking up your Bible again might sound like work. This can lead to burnout, which happens when your public activities override your private intimacy with God.

When you're both exhausted and deprived of God's Word, it can begin to affect all other areas of your life. You're starving yourself. You might start to become indecisive, impatient with co-workers, or worried and afraid. Instead of casting your cares onto God and trusting Him, you might try to pick them up and figure them out on your own. You might start carrying things you weren't even meant to carry.

When this happens, remember that reading the Word gives you strength. The Bible is the Bread of Life.

It is important to dive into and read the Bible for yourself and not only rely on listening to sermons and the interpretations of others. I used to depend fully on what other people had to say and what my friends told me about the Word. As I mentioned previously, I didn't start reading the Bible for myself until I was living in Dubai. I had spiritual anorexia and didn't even know it! It wasn't until after I started consuming the Bread of Life that I realized how much I had been starving myself. I started by reading a translation of the Bible that was easier to understand, followed by a study Bible, which helped me to apply the scripture to my life.

If you feel that you are currently suffering from spiritual anorexia, here are some steps and suggestions to follow that will help you overcome it:

- **Get a Bible.** If you don't already have one, I encourage you to find a Bible that you can read and understand. There are many translations that can be found at your local or Christian bookstore, church, online, or at conferences. I personally love the *Life Application Study Bible NLT*. I love the commentary and how it really digs into the characters, has maps of the locations, and shares examples of how to apply the scriptures to your daily life.

This is significant because just reading the Bible isn't enough. Even demons know the Word and tremble in His presence (James 2:19). But it is your life that separates this truth and the light that you carry. Let your lifestyle speak to others, not your "knowledge" of the Bible.

Initially when I read the Bible, I would fall asleep. Why? I don't talk the way they do in the Bible, and I needed help understanding the scriptures. The Holy Spirit will lead and guide you in the understanding, but I love this particular version because it gives you examples of how to effectively apply what you are learning to your everyday life. I also love the *NIV Bible* and the *Joyce Meyer Bible*. Find the one that works best for you! In doing this, I suggest going to your local bookstore and checking out different translations. You can even speak to your pastor or your family and friends and ask what translation they use.

- **Schedule time each day to read your Bible.** Just like with any other relationship, we must cultivate and make conscious time to feed our spirit with the Word of God. We need to make it a priority above all things. There is no right or wrong way to study the Word, and there is no certain amount of time you must spend reading each day — just go with what your spirit is telling you. I chose to read my Bible from beginning to end, but you can start wherever the Lord leads you first. Taking time to read and reflect on God's Word each day is what's most important. If you're just beginning, I recommend starting with the Gospels of Matthew, Mark, Luke, and John to lay a foundation. Then, continue with 1 John, 2 John, 3 John, Acts, Romans, 1 Corinthians, and the rest of the New Testament. Reading through the Old Testament is just as essential, but you likely will have more clarity when reading it if you go through the New Testament first.

The importance of spending time with God applies on your good days just as much as it does on your bad days. When things are going well, don't assume that you can stop seeking God! It is important to continuously pursue Him.

- **Take note of what stands out to you.** As you're reading the Bible, notice the scriptures that speak to you. I love highlighting and writing in mine. I also like to journal about what I feel Him saying to me, and then I journal what I want to say back to Him. Another idea is to write down on notecards the scriptures that you want to remember. I love doing this! Sometimes I add my name to the scripture so it can be more personal. For example, instead of writing, "For I know the plans I have for you says the Lord," I write, "Juliette, I know the plans I have for you. Plans to prosper you, give you hope, and a future" (Jeremiah 29:11). There is no right or wrong way to study the Bible and talk to God! Do whatever works for you and helps you strengthen your relationship with Him.

- **Join a Bible study group.** It is important for us to be accountable to someone in our journey and walk with God. This might seem scary at first because it will require you to be honest with yourself and others about where you're at in your faith. You likely will be stretched and challenged, but that is how you grow. Joining a Bible study also will help you in building a community and in forming Godly, encouraging relationships. If you don't have a Bible-teaching church where you can attend bible study, I encourage you to look into organizations like The Pinky Promise Movement, which is an organization of women from all over the world whose mission is to honor God with their lives and bodies. There are global small groups that meet bi-weekly to do Bible studies and fun gatherings. You can even start your own group!

Jesus died so that we could be saved through trusting in Him. He died to have a deep and personal relationship with each one of us. He loves you with an unconditional love, despite all of your flaws. In Deuteronomy 31:6, He promises that He will never leave nor forsake you. He is with you every day, but this relationship can't be one-sided. You must spend time with Him for your relationship to flourish and to avoid falling into the trap of spiritual anorexia.

When you feed your spirit with His Word, you will mature in your identity in Christ. You will become more in-tune with how

He speaks to you and what He desires of you on this earth. People will know you and associate you with Jesus by the fruit in your life (Matthew 7:16). You will develop love, joy, peace, patience, kindness, goodness, faithfulness, gentleness, and self-control, which all are fruits of the spirit as stated in Galatians 5:22-23. When you are spiritually fit and strong, you will be able to hear God's voice and respond to His call to step out in faith.

Chapter 6:

FAITH IN THE SINGLE SEASON

Maybe you're reading this and thinking, "Okay, that's great and all, but I'm single. What if God is calling me to move to a place where there aren't any men that I like? My clock is ticking, and I need to think about my future."

Maybe you're approaching 30, or another big milestone, and everyone around you is asking you why you're still single with no kids. What did you dream of accomplishing by this age in life? Maybe you wanted to be married, have kids, have a million dollars in the bank, or even to know that you have found Mr. Right... right? Ha. Yeah, the American dream.

What happened to the belief that God knows what's best for us? He is the Creator of all things. He chose us in such a special way that He knows the number of hairs on our heads, right? Or is that only for married people with kids? Many people "fear" getting older because they start to think of what they don't have or where they wish they were in life.

Maybe you feel as if you don't have a purpose or that you're not living in your purpose? Maybe you're waiting on God's promises to come to fruition? Whatever the reason may be, I just want you to know that **God's timing is not always our timing.** *At the right time, God has a way of taking the world's idea of perfection and blowing it right out of the water with His promises for your life.* Although I don't have a husband and children yet, I am expectant and excited to see what my Heavenly Father is preparing me for.

It's easy to get caught up in comparing your journey with the journeys of others. However, that seed will grow into dangerous envy and jealousy for things we *think* we desire. The Bible shows us that when we reduce ourselves to comparing our lives and accomplishments to others, we end up fighting a battle that we were never made for. If you need someone to compare your life to, look toward the people in the Bible. There are many examples that will edify you in whatever season you are in.

The age 30 is actually a *significant* age in the Bible. It demonstrates the impossible being made possible through God's authority.

Here are some examples:

- Jesus started His ministry at 30 (Luke 3:23).
- David became King at 30 (2 Samuel 5:4).
- Joseph stepped out of his wilderness season and become second to Pharaoh at 30 (Genesis 41:46).
- Ezekiel was called by God as a prophet at age 30 (Ezekiel 1:1).
- John the Baptist was 30 when he came out from the wilderness to pave the way for the Messiah (Jesus).

As you can see, 30 is *the bomb* age in the Bible. We should be celebrating the significance of growing into our destinies, not sulking and being depressed while trying to figure out what's next. People stepped into their purpose at this age, so if you are not sure what is going on, *it's okay!* **Let your hope be in the Word and God's promises, not in the world and its promises.**

So, what did I do on my 30th birthday? I actually was on a plane leaving Cape Town, South Africa, heading to America. Yes, I was on a plane for my birthday. I was leaving what had been my home for the last three years to start my transition back to life in Atlanta — the place God was sending me for my next season.

Before I left, many people were saying, "Wow, you are flying on your birthday? That sucks!" Well, actually, it didn't — that time was significant for me. Our purpose on this earth is to glorify God, and it was an honor to fly on my birthday. It represented so many things to me. I was stepping into a new season, age, and destination. I wouldn't have changed that day for anything. I also wasn't just traveling, but I was stepping out in faith. I left my life, friends, job, and church family to step into the unknown. I didn't know what this next season held for me, but I knew the One who held it in His hands.

I actually know of someone who locked themselves up in their room and didn't leave their house on their 30th birthday because they felt they were not where they wanted to be when the clock struck midnight. That's not okay. Age doesn't determine specific milestones for success. **True success is walking in God's will for your life, and that is at *any* age!** We have to be in-tune and close to God to know exactly what that looks like for us.

When you spend a lot of time with your friends and family, you *know* them — their desires, likes, and dislikes. The same is true with God. As you seek Him and spend time with him, you will know Him. You will soon have the convictions and peace to go and do what He wants you to do. **Seek the kingdom of God above all else and everything will be added unto you.**

Leading up to my 30th birthday, I did a daily video countdown. Maybe you're thinking, "Okay, a countdown? What were you excited for?" Normally you do a countdown when you have it all together and are excited to celebrate something new. The world's standards could cause one to hide themselves like a turtle in their shell. I was putting myself out there in the complete opposite way, without the world's care. I was celebrating the courage to step out into the unknown by faith alone. I didn't know exactly where I was going or how I would get there, but I just trusted God, and He carried me through it all.

Never allow your age, friends, family, or anyone else to determine where you "should" be in your life. If God had considered age, why didn't He use Jesus earlier in life? After all, He was the chosen Messiah. Maybe God knew Jesus's life would have been taken and the promise would have not been accomplished. God demonstrates His love to keep us from certain situations for our protection.

When you are ready, whatever you desire will be directed by God, and you will be so thankful you didn't rush His will for your life. Rejoice in knowing that you're protected, loved, and guided by the Most High, Jesus Christ.

It's the peace that surpasses all understanding that confirms when you are in the right place.

"But those who hope in the Lord will renew their strength. They will soar on wings like eagles; they will run and not grow weary, they will walk and not be faint." – Isaiah 40:31

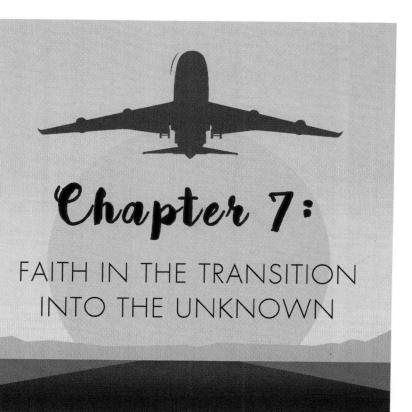

Chapter 7:

FAITH IN THE TRANSITION
INTO THE UNKNOWN

Has God ever told you to move without giving you a clear picture of where He's taking you? You might be thinking, "God is calling me to make the jump, but I have no idea where to!" That was me when I left South Africa.

As I was on the plane on my 30th birthday, I had no idea what I was going to do. Yes, I was flying back to Atlanta, but I wasn't headed toward a job or a paycheck. Two weeks before I left Cape Town, I reached out to my friend who lives there and told her that I was coming back. She told me that she had been praying for an assistant for help in her ministry, non-profit, and online store. When I first called her, I had no idea that she needed any help or that she would consider me to fill that need for her!

Upon agreeing to be her assistant, I didn't expect to make any money because it was still ministry. I was so excited for the opportunity, but I still thought to myself, "This is America! How am I going to do this?! Everything is on another level when it comes to expenses and finances."

I knew I potentially could get a paying part-time job and also work for her, but I didn't really want to. I knew that would cause me to give 50 percent as her assistant and 50 percent to the part-time job, so I prayed and trusted God that He would work this out however He saw fit.

Before I left South Africa, my friends there prayed for me and stood by me in my transition to this next season. I didn't leave Cape Town because my funds were low. I didn't leave Cape Town because I didn't like my job. I didn't leave Cape

Town because I had no friends. **I left because the Lord was telling me to go.** He was shifting me into a new season. I asked God who would be affected by my obedience. I began to strategize ways that my position, the roles I carried, and the tasks I was responsible for would continue to flow productively in my absence.

Before I got on the plane, I had so many doubts about doing full-time ministry in the States. The enemy was telling me, "People will think that you are lazy," and "It won't be the same as South Africa," and "It's not going to work out." It wasn't until I stepped on that plane on December 25th that I felt the full peace that surpassed all understanding. That's when I knew everything would fall into place.

When I arrived in Atlanta, I started serving right away. Of course, being an assistant isn't always structured and black and white. Things came up unexpectedly, and my tasks were different each day. I prayed for the ability to do things right, and that's what the Lord graced me to do. **There were times I had no idea how to do a task, but the Lord gave me the wisdom I needed to see it through.**

One of the goals I wrote down as I was coming back to America was to cook more and to be more intentional about my health. My friend is a vegetarian and cooks almost all of her meals, so this was an area that I was able to be intentional about and focus on during my time as an assistant. From going vegan for a month to becoming a full-blown vegetarian, God truly blew me away with how he answered the desires of my heart. Serving in that role and being in that environment on a daily basis influenced my health for the better. I learned to cook meals I didn't even know existed, while also being stretched spiritually. Serving unto the Lord also released my friend's capacity to do other things and allowed her businesses to grow in many other areas.

I had no expectation of compensation when I arrived, but she gave me weekly money for gas and provided meals during my work days, as well as extra money as God led her. Within a few months, a position was created for me! God provided for her and her business, which allowed for Him to also provide for me. Within a month, I took on the role as store manager of her online boutique. Eventually, I became her booking manager. This gave me the opportunity to travel around the world with her for speaking engagements. *How good is God?!* I *love* to travel. I never even asked for this position, but He really fulfills the desires of our hearts if we let Him. My friend thought me being here was a blessing to her, but she has hands down has been a blessing to me as well.

The Lord gave me instruction to just *rest*. I don't know where will be next, but I'm committed to taking it day by day. I didn't want to be in America just getting by; I wanted to live in abundance and also be a blessing to others. God has provided for me to do just that. As I have rested in Him, He has graced me in my tasks. He gave me this analogy: When we transfer from elementary to middle school as children, we don't worry about school supplies, transportation, or the food we will eat. We just go and know that our transition and season will be covered. That is exactly what He has done for me. He had this season planned when I was in my mother's womb.

Just a few weeks after I arrived in Atlanta, my friend asked me to be a speaker at her upcoming annual women's conference. I was shocked! I didn't tell anyone initially because I was afraid she might change her mind. I didn't think I was capable of speaking at a conference! I probably felt a lot like Moses did when the Lord asked him to speak, but I trusted that God would give me the words to say as He called me to this position.

She had already lined up her speakers the year before, so there was not a slot for me. Instead of her speaking twice, I would be taking one of her slots. She wanted me to teach on walking by faith.

I wasn't on her radar at first. She wasn't even thinking of me for the conference. **If God has a plan for you to speak somewhere, He will lay it on people's hearts.** *This wasn't significant to me because she asked me, but it was significant because the Holy Spirit told her.* This was a defining moment and confirmation that I was where I was supposed to be.

I just want to encourage you not to run if an opportunity comes your way and you find yourself thinking, "But, I'm not ready yet!" The best things in life generally come when we least expect them to. We have to be ready and prepared just to do it!

In fact, amazing opportunities tend to come when we don't think we're ready. *Yes,* you may feel nervous. *Yes,* you may feel unqualified. *Yes,* you may not feel ready. **You have to let God move.**

I'm sharing this story with you because I want you to know that you were born ready. God knows the right timing for opportunities and open doors in your life. Be discerning and pray before making a big decision, but **do not let "fear" stop you from stepping out.**

There are so many times that I didn't have all the answers, but God provided. I have already shared several in this book, but I want to share a couple more testimonies to really encourage you in how detailed and specific He is when taking care of us.

God loves to spoil and surprise you:

I didn't have a steady cash flow when I first arrived in Atlanta, but the Lord provided for me. I really wanted to get my hair done during the first few months I was there, but I couldn't afford it. One day I said, "Lord, I would just love to get my hair done." That same week, one of my friends randomly messaged me saying she wanted to bless me with a hair appointment at the salon of my choice. I chose the salon I've always wanted to visit. The Lord is so faithful! He loves to spoil and surprise us!

God provides at 40,000 feet:

When I boarded a plane to fly overseas and serve at a ministry event in London, I only had $7 in my bank account. I said, "Lord, the trains will have to cost 50 cents or something. How are we going to get around?" Upon landing at my layover in Doha, someone *on the plane* gave me $75 and told me, "I don't want to sound weird, but the Lord told me to give this to you."

When I tell you the Lord provides, He *provides!* Whether you are 40,000 feet up in the air wondering how you will pay for transportation, running low on funds a day before your rent is due, or are looking at the lack of food in your fridge in the middle of the month and don't know how you will make it until your next payday, He never fails and will *always* come through for you!

"And my God will meet all your needs according to the riches of his glory in Christ Jesus." – Philippians 4:19

We will never arrive at trusting God. It's a constant journey, but one well worth the destination. I want to encourage you to continue to do what God is calling you to do — even if you're scared, don't have all the answers, or don't know how things will come into fruition. **God will move as you move.** If God is telling you to move now, then *move*. If God is telling you to start a new job, then put in that application! You may not understand it all right away, but know this: *"His thoughts are not your thoughts, neither is ways your ways"* (Isaiah 55:8).

His promises are true. He will never leave you. In Joshua 1:9, he commands: *"Be strong and courageous. Do not be afraid; do not be discouraged for the Lord your God will be with you wherever you go."*

He will send people to support you. He will never forsake you. He is with you each step of the way.

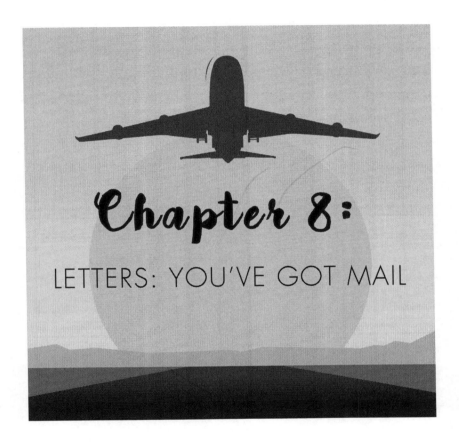

Chapter 8:

LETTERS: YOU'VE GOT MAIL

Reading and hearing stories of how God's promises were fulfilled in other's lives is something that has always encouraged me in my faith journey. The following are numerous testimonies written by individuals from all over the world who have answered God's call to step out in faith. I personally know each of them, and I can attest to their faith, strength, and courage. Just like Paul wrote to the church, these Holy Spirit led letters are intended to encourage you in the season you're in.

"The disciples saw Jesus do many miraculous signs in addition to the ones recorded in this book. But these are written so that you can continue to believe Jesus is the Messiah, the Son of God, and that by believing in him you will have life by the power of his name." – John 21:30-31 (NLT)

The Great Unknown: From Cape Town, South Africa, to the UK

Knowing God and trusting God are two very different things. Unfortunately, most believers only ever know God, and few actually discover his true nature as a good, good Father. For those who welcome a relationship with God, stepping into the glorious unknown is one of the scariest, yet most fulfilling adventures.

While serving God in South Africa, and having been under incredible leaders in our amazing church in Cape Town, my family embarked on that adventure. We felt God speaking to us, with instruction to go and pioneer a Church in the United Kingdom. We had no resources, no salaries, no home, no covering; just a promise, *"I will never leave you, nor forsake you"* (Deuteronomy 31:6). Through this journey, I have come to realize that one promise from God is worth more than one thousand opinions from others.

Reflecting back on our time in Cape Town, I realized God took me through three major tests to prepare me for the task of pioneering SOUL Church UK, in Norwich. I believe these three tests are challenges every emerging leader will face before launching into the deep.

Test 1 - God is your SOURCE - God wants to be sure we are fully dependent on him. Often he allows us to go through lean seasons so we can place our trust in him alone. We didn't receive a salary the first 12 months of our journey in South Africa, but we trusted God with our every need. Can I encourage you? Do not look to a person, a business man, or a family member to be your source. God is the source of everything you need. Direct your prayers and needs to Him, and you will never lack any good thing.

Test 2 - God is SOVEREIGN - How do we respond when life doesn't play along? In 2010, I received a call that my dad only had a few weeks to live with leukemia. My world stopped. Sometimes there will be questions unanswered this side of eternity, but what is our response when bad things happen to good people? I believe the answer to this test is coming to a place in our hearts where we say, "Do I understand? No. Do I trust you God? Yes." As painful as that season was in my life, it taught me that God is sovereign when my trust is truly in Him.

Test 3 - Godly SUBMISSION - How do we respond under authority? We will never successfully be in positions of leadership until we fully submit under the authority of the

Father. The final test for a leader is submitting to Godly authority, even when we don't agree with the decision or leadership style. How we serve another vision ultimately determines how someone one day will serve ours.

God has never failed us, and He won't start now.
The best is yet to come.

Jon Norman
soulchurch.com

Leaving Corporate: From Australia to Cape Town, South Africa

I have always sensed that I was called to ministry of some sort, but I was afraid of what that may look like. Instead, I chose to study accounting; not because I was passionate about it, or even because my personality in any way suits that kind of work, but because it was safe. Changing the world seemed great in theory, but not so great when I couldn't logically figure out how it would pay my bills. Isn't it funny how fear often masks itself as wisdom? We can always talk ourselves into living timidly by labeling it as "smart," and that's exactly what I did.

I was frustrated because I knew I was going against what felt natural to me and how God really created me to function. I reached the peak of my frustration a year into my job as a Tax Accountant. Not only did I not like what I was doing, but I also was not allowing myself the opportunity to discover what it was God really created me to do.

I quit my job not knowing what to do next, but I knew that being an accountant wasn't what I was going to do for the rest of my life. Many people didn't understand my decision, and I didn't expect them to. Why would you study for four years, be privileged enough to get a job in your field, and then quit because you don't feel "called to it?" It didn't make sense at the time, and not all faith decisions do, but sometimes faith requires that you walk alone for a season.

I worked in retail for a year, and then I moved to Cape Town, South Africa, to participate in a Leadership Development Program at Hillsong Church. I didn't necessarily hear the voice of God tell me to go to Hillsong Cape Town, but I took the step of faith believing that, through this, I would discover what God called me to do and would have a clearer idea of how I could channel my gifts to advance His kingdom. Many times I wondered if I was making wrong decisions or taking wrong turns, but one thing I did know was that the life I had been living was not the life I wanted; I had to know what was on the other side of my fear.

God opened so many ministry opportunities for me in Cape Town. I regularly facilitated personal development workshops for women, had the opportunity to teach Bible College, and received my first invitation as a guest speaker at a women's conference. I remember moments where I thought, "This is what God was thinking when He created me!" God exceeded my expectations! I also experienced the financial provision of God — never lacking in want or need. My life has never been the same. Something happens when you step out in faith and begin to see the miraculous hand of God respond to your faith. One of the great heroes of faith, Smith Wigglesworth, said this: "If God doesn't move me, I'll move Him." I believe that faith always touches the heart of God; when we move towards Him, He can't help but move towards us.

The reward of faith isn't so much that you suddenly get everything you have ever wanted, or that everything you do from now on magically works because you dared to step out and do something radical for God. For me, the reward of faith has been better than that. It's the surge of life that I feel rushing through my soul every time I have an opportunity to express the glory of God through the gifts He has given me. My reward is that I am finally free — free from the limitations of fear! I am free to influence the world with the mind of Christ, knowing that God is with me.

Faith is knowing that God is the source of all provision; not a job or a person — only God! Abraham was willing to lay His son at the altar because he reasoned that the God who gave Him the promise was also able to raise his son from the dead. He trusted the One who promised more than the need to hold onto his son, through whom the promise would come. I am not afraid to say no to opportunities or to walk away from something I think I need because everything I need is in God, for "In Him I love, and move, and have my being."

I pray that you will be encouraged to step out and do what God has put on your heart to do, and that your courage would grow with each step of faith that you take. I pray that you will experience the love of God through your encounter with Him, and that His love will set you free from the limitations that fear has placed on your life. What is keeping you from doing what God is calling you to? What is on the other side of your fears? I dare you to the first step to find out!

"And may the Lord our God show us his approval and make our efforts successful. Yes, make our efforts successful!" –Psalm 90:17 (ESV)

Romayne Jay
theesteemproject.com

The Great Unknown:
From State to State

As I sat down to write this letter, I couldn't help but think about how faithful God is to His children. I honestly know that it is only by the grace of God that I am still here. You see, four years ago while I was living in NYC, I prayed a dangerous prayer, asking The Lord to give me faith like Abraham, courage like Joshua, and wisdom like Solomon. I had no idea what that would entail, but I was tired of feeling unfulfilled with my "play it safe" mentality. I knew that God wanted more of me and that I needed to fully surrender my life to Him. I never thought that would mean God would call me to move not once, but twice, in less than three years. I honestly thought that when I said "yes" to God and moved to Atlanta, then that would be the end of my faith walk. This couldn't have been further from the truth. I've come to realize that as a servant of The Lord I must go wherever the Master sends me and fulfill whatever assignment He has for me there.

On January 2, 2016, I left EVERYTHING behind in Atlanta, Georgia, and moved to Dallas, Texas. At the time, I did not have a job, any source of income, or a bunch of money in my savings account; I just knew that God wanted me to go. So I packed up whatever could fit in my little compact car and drove by myself to the place that God had shown me. I've been here for six months trekking through what I call the "wilderness," and God has been faithful through it all.

Even though I didn't work for almost two months, I never went without. I've learned that God is truly the provider of my daily bread. My joy, peace, hope, contentment, and strength are found in Him alone. There are some lessons that can only be learned as we go through the fire. Although I don't always understand God's ways, what I do know is that He is trustworthy and sovereign. I don't know what God has in store for me next, but I do know that because I have endured this season, I will be grateful and prepared for whatever may come.

God has not called us to live a life that is safe and predictable. He has called us to live a life in which risks are taken, mountains are moved, and captives are set free. He has created us to follow Him — no matter the cost, no matter where He leads, and no matter how uncomfortable it is. You were designed to glorify God and to proclaim His goodness to the nations. In order to grow, your faith must be tested. God desires that you step out of your boat and into the waters. If you play it safe, you will never experience all that He has written in His book for you. It will not always be fun or easy, but do not grow weary in well doing.

When others do not understand and ridicule you, remember that God is on your side. With Him, ALL things are possible. When life doesn't go as you planned, keep your eyes on Jesus, the author and finisher of your faith. It is He that will finish the good work that He started in you. Walking by faith does not always equate to moving. There are many ways that God may challenge us to let go of what we can see and trade it for the unknown. My prayer is that whatever God is asking of you right now, you would be faithful to walk in obedience and fulfill the destiny that He has tailored just for you. Christ didn't halfway die on the cross for us, so let's not halfway live for Him here on this earth.

"I can do ALL things through Christ who strengthens me."
- Philippians 4:13 (NKJV)

"For we walk by FAITH, not by sight."
- 2 Corinthians 5:7 (NKJV)

Cierra Cotton
Cierracotton.blogspot.com

Creative Design to God's Design:
From the Philippines to Cape Town,
South Africa

When I was choosing a field to study in college, I told God I wanted an exciting career that would impact a massive audience. He didn't reply to my plea with large neon signs, but instead gave me another thought. I felt in my heart that one day I would do something radical and crazy for him. I didn't know what it meant or what that would look like. I never really took it seriously, and I went on and pursued advertising.

True enough, I found myself in a promising career of consumerism, marketing, and graphic design. I enjoyed my creative job in making commercials until, one day, after a long and frustrating client meeting, I realized that I was burned out, lost, and confused with where my life had gone and where was headed. In my heart, I knew I was meant for something more.

I tried to navigate through that season of confusion and search for direction, and I ended up deciding to go to Bible College in Sydney. At first, it looked like things were lining up. However, while I was preparing myself for the big move, God closed that door. I was confused and didn't understand what God was doing. In the quest for answers, I continued to trust God and fought off my fears and doubts. I was convinced God wanted to pull me out of my situation.

During this period of discernment, a missionary friend of mine told me about a church in South Africa. I was not really so keen about it because I wanted to study in Australia. I felt moving Africa was too much and too crazy for me. To my surprise, after finding out about their internship program I was brave enough to answer, "YES" to the question, "Are you willing to give a year of your life to build God's house?"

Without hesitation, I quit my job. I left my life in the Philippines and answered God's call to South Africa. Coming into a place of the unknown with no friends or family and limited finances was indeed the craziestand most radical thing I've done in my life.

I didn't know what my life would look like or how I would survive. God revealed to me His characteristics in ways I could've never imagined. He showed me how to love others genuinely by placing me in challenging situations. He revealed His compassionate heart by stretching me outside my comfort zone through praying for people on the street and visiting and encouraging the sick in public clinics. God demonstrated pure joy and fun to me through the smiles of the kids we serve in our programs. Whenever financial struggles came, God spoke through the homeless people we serve and proved to me that He can and will always provide.

Oftentimes, our personal ambitions can take over God's plans for our lives. My case might be different than yours. What matters most is that God knows the real case of your heart. If we only listen and take that brave step of faith through obedience and submission, He will perform wonders that cannot be fathomed. The miracles that you will experience cannot be counted.

In the end, God answered my plea. He has given me a job that is far from boring, and the major difference is that now I know I am making an impact for Jesus to the ends of the earth.

Norbert Elnar
masterpiecemovement.com

Faith in Action:
From Comfort to the Unknown

Faith is not a figment of one's imagination. It is not a fairytale told over centuries. It is the very evidence of what we hope for even though we do not see it. It is the essence to life — the key that unlocks eternal value and life. It is by faith that we can trust in Jesus and receive the Holy Spirit. We must come to the conclusion on faith. It is the single most important element of our lives; therefore, it is a priority to walk by it and live in it. It is the only way to live.

I started my life of faith back in 2005 when I truly came to Christ. He drew me in with love, and I like to tell others that I came to Him kicking and screaming. It was at the altar that I laid down my burdens. It was only about a year later that I would lose everything completely to follow Him. I dropped out of college and left everything behind. I was in a place where I had nothing or no one to hold onto except God. I had to trust Him. Those were lonely days, but I needed all of them. They made me into the man I am today. After almost a year of petitioning Heaven for my next orders, I finally heard God tell me that it was time for me to move into my next stage of training. That training ground was employment at a church. I worked there for almost four years until I resigned to go into full-time ministry. No, I did not have a job on the side. I did not have a degree to boast on or hang on my wall. All I had was a word from God, and I had to learn that it was all I needed.

After resigning from my job, my wife and I moved to Jackson, Mississippi. We were newly married living in a new state surrounded by new people with new orders from God. Our faith was tested daily. We had to learn what it meant to live on daily bread. That is when you trust that God will provide the next meal. We had to learn to trust that He will teach you what you need to know and give you the wisdom when you do not know what to do. We tried everything we could to be proactive and do ministry work, but nothing seemed to work. After almost two years of being in Jackson, my wife and I moved back to Atlanta, Georgia. It was there that we planted a church, The Gathering Oasis Church, after almost a year after we moved.

Throughout the many years of my life of faith, I have learned many things. One of those important lessons is to never go ahead of God. Oftentimes, we try to move quicker than Him. We try to make things happen that do not need to happen in that season. Because we live in a "fast-food culture" we expect everything to be delivered quickly, but God does not always work that way. He moves as He pleases, and He fully expects for you to patiently wait until it is time.

I have learned to trust His pruning. He is the Holy Gardener, and His work is always fair. He prunes as He chooses, and He does it as He wishes. Trust Him when things change and relationships do not go as you think they should without any evil doing on your part. He subtracts, adds, multiples, and divides as He wills. Trust Him in the process.

I have also learned to be content, and that can be our greatest challenge. I encourage you to be content no matter if you have little or much. God is a great provider. You can always trust Him. You can lean on Him. You can rest in Him. And you must always serve Him. Now, go in faith, and run your race well.

Cornelius Lindsey
corneliuslindsey.com

Chapter 9:
WRITE, BABY, WRITE

Each one of us has a testimony, and it is our assignment on earth to share our story with others. That can be done through a blog, a book, a magazine, or by public speaking. It is our responsibility to share what we have gone through and the wisdom God has given us in order to uplift, inspire, and encourage others to further God's kingdom.

If you think about it, the Bible is filled with testimonies. Each book lays down a significant testimony, starting with the words spoken by God to create the earth in Genesis. Examples include: Sarah bearing a child in old age when she thought she couldn't have one (Genesis 21:2); the Apostle Paul prevailing and sustaining through his suffering (2 Corinthians 11); Joseph trusting God and forgiving his family after being mocked, beaten, and sold into slavery (Genesis 50:17); and Noah being laughed at by those around him for building an ark (Genesis 5:32-10:1). Without all of the testimonies in God's Word, where would our comfort come from in times of distress? These stories attest to God's amazing faithfulness, promises, and works.

God wants you to tell your story, too. Telling your story reveals that God is still alive and working in people's lives today. I'm not suggesting that everyone reading this has a book or a blog that they're meant to write at this exact moment, but that we should be open with what God has done in our lives. Maybe you're just starting to step out in faith. Maybe there's something you're presently working to overcome. Maybe you're currently walking in the middle of the testimony that God has planned for you to share. If that is the case, you can return to this chapter and use it both as a guide and an encouragement whenever and however God leads you; but be encouraged to use your life as a living testimony to the power of God that has worked through you.

The following tips and suggestions are meant to help you think about, form, and share the story that God has placed on your heart.

- **Don't listen to the enemy.** First things first: Before you even put your pen to the paper, the enemy will try to deter you from sharing what God has put in your heart. Even with this book, the enemy tried to kill the passion that I had to bring it to fruition. When one of my editors provided her first constructive feedback, I became paralyzed. She was just doing her job, but the enemy was trying to use that. I instantly felt like I was not enough and that my work didn't matter, wasn't significant, and didn't make sense. It was hard for me to go back to the drawing board again because I was discouraged and overwhelmed. Looking back at it now, I was just overthinking it.

  Once I recognized that the enemy was trying to steal the calling God had for me in this book, it made me go write with passion to finish what He had already started in me.

- **Journal your thoughts.** Even if you think a book is way off your radar, journaling is a great way to practice putting your thoughts to paper and making sense of them. Journaling gives you an opportunity to sit and reflect on the ways you are growing in your faith and the things that God is doing in your life. This could be written in any form, or you could record your thoughts and transcribe them later. Do whatever works for you! Find a method that really gets your creative juices flowing. Personally, I love to journal on my laptop. I find this makes it easier to categorize my notes and writing. I also don't have the best handwriting, so typing makes it easier for me to read it back to myself.

- **Reach out to someone.** Writing a book might sound like a daunting task; but if you can speak it, you can write it. During my own writing journey, I have noticed that when you step out in faith and decide to write a book, God will align the right people in your path to help you. You will be graced.

- **Become familiar with free blogging tools.** If you decide to set up a blog, I suggest using a free hosting site. When I first began my blog, I thought it was difficult to use the platforms. Just like with anything we wish to master, it takes practice. Reach out to people who may know more than you and ask questions. In fact, one of my friends initially built my site for me, and I eventually got the hang of it by continuously posting!

- **Practice writing.** Offering to write for someone else can be a great way to practice and improve your writing skills. During my second year of the community outreach internship in Cape Town, I wanted to expand my voice and writing. I began writing for the program's Sisterhood blog and internship site. Think about who or what you might like to write for. Maybe it could be a publication at your school, a church blog, a work website, or a local newspaper. Maybe you could offer to help someone else write their own testimony or story! There likely are many opportunities around you. Don't be shy about seeking them out.

  Another way you could strengthen your writing and also build community is by joining a writers club. If there isn't one around you, start one! You could share writings such as poetry, songs, short stories, or testimonies. You could learn from each other and build an encouraging community.

- **Be led by the Lord.** Whether you plan to post once a week or once a month, don't be too hard on yourself if you're not publishing as often as you would like. Don't post something just to post it, and don't force yourself to write empty words when you just want to fill a quota you set for yourself. Be Holy Spirit led in everything you write and share.

If you see someone else posting every week, don't compare. Stay in your own lane. God will have the right eyes for your post.

I remember once when I was blogging regularly, I wanted to share something but God didn't lead me to share at that time. An entire year went by, and still I didn't post because I didn't feel led to. Anyone else would think I would lose subscribers or followers because I stopped posting. The first time I posted after my "hiatus," I had over 40,000 views in my first week! When I made that post, I had a conviction from God to do so. Let this encourage you not post things "just because." The impact will come when you are led by God. This also applies when you write your book. Don't write a book just because you feel you should, but think about why you really want to write one. What is God pressing on your heart to share? How will He be glorified?

- **Trust God with the resources.** Is a lack of resources, such as a computer or internet access, keeping you from writing? Don't let it! If you don't have internet at your residence, find a coffee shop nearby. If you don't have a laptop or computer, ask a friend to borrow theirs. One of my friends has a major blog and recently wrote her first book, all without having her own computer! She trusted that God would provide for her, and she was able to write and post when visiting friends that had computers.

Don't let small obstacles like these stand in the way. Don't let them deter you from starting and completing what God has put in you. Continue to trust God to provide the resources needed for the work that He has entrusted you with. It will all come to fruition as you persevere and rely on Him.

- **Find an editor or proofreader.** If you're not confident in your writing skills, have someone you trust and respect proofread your work and provide constructive feedback. Even if you are confident, it's always helpful to have a second pair of eyes. Ask them to walk alongside you in the journey. This does not mean that they should do the work for you. Make time to take note of any suggestions they give for the construction, grammar, spelling, and flow of your writing. This will help you improve your skills so that you can master those mistakes and avoid making them again in the future.

- **Be you.** There is no right or wrong in writing and sharing your story. Each person has their own unique voice. God made us all different. Don't try to sound or be like anyone else. Don't compare yourself to anyone else. Be the you that God created you to be.

- **Remember why you're writing.** Don't become too focused on who or how many people are watching your site. Don't worry too much about whether or not your readers will like what you're sharing. I have struggled with these thoughts myself, and they actually prolonged the creation of my site Jules The Explorer (julestheexplorer.com). I started the blog to encourage young Americans to travel, and I had so many fresh ideas of how I was going to execute it. I was excited, but I also was still insecure about sharing it with the world. Even though the site was finished, I would let it sit for weeks while trying to perfect it. When I finally published it, I took it down within 20 minutes when no one liked it on social media. I deleted the post and didn't share my site because I was afraid that no one cared.

I went on with my life with the site in the back of my head, knowing that I would publish it again someday. I was going to wait until I had the confidence to do it. I later discovered that someone else had started a blog using the same theme and creative ideas as mine. This made me realize that God was going to get His message across, whether it was through me or someone else. I was disappointed in myself for not publishing my blog the first time God laid it on my heart. When I did finally publish it, following through with God's ideas gave me great confidence and reassurance that I was on the right track. It encouraged me to obey immediately next time He gave me creative ideas. It reminded me to go for the like of Christ, not the likes on social media.

Remember that you're sharing your story because God laid it on your heart. He already knows who it is meant to reach, and He will direct the right set of eyes to your writing. Base your confidence in Him and not in the opinions of others.

We are called to be the salt of the earth. We are called to be a light – a bright light shining on a lamp post on top of a hill (Matthew 5:3-16). God will use your testimony to reach and help someone else — it is meant to be shared. A story about how God helped you overcome something could give someone else the strength, wisdom, and courage to overcome something similar they're going through. Maybe it will help them realize that they're not alone. After reading your testimony, they might relate to it and think, "If God did it for them, He can do it for me."

Do not underestimate the power of your testimony. Revelation 12:11 says:

"And they have defeated him by the blood of the lamb and by their testimony." (NLT)

Chapter 10:

DON'T QUIT

I truly hope that all of the testimonies and stories in this book have inspired you to step out in faith. You do not have to be anywhere near perfect to do what God is calling you to do. I am far from having it all together; I don't have a PhD on faith, and I don't sit on the right hand of our Father, but I can attest to what He has fulfilled in my life. I wrote this book to let you know that if God can do it for me, He can do it for you. This book has no one in mind but you. I wish someone would have told me these things as I was navigating my journey, and this is my motivation for sharing all that God has placed on my heart with so much conviction. I believe sharing your testimony to encourage others is just as important as the action of stepping out in faith.

Once you answer God's call, I also want to encourage you not to quit in the process. Keep pushing. Don't listen to the voices of people who may try to deter you. Find your strength, hope, joy, direction, and peace in the Lord. Being in Christ means not being a slave to this world, but being free in Him — free to do what He has called you to do. You can fly and have faith that God will catch you if you stumble or fall. He will keep you safely under His wings through it all.

If God has called you to step out in faith in an extraordinary way, remember not to think that you've "made it." Don't think that you have "arrived" and that there isn't any more room to grow.

"Make a careful exploration of who you are and the work you have been given, and then sink yourself into that. Don't be impressed with yourself. Don't compare yourself with others."
– Galatians 6:10 (The Message)

I love how this verse states, "Don't be impressed with yourself." When we look at ourselves in our own strength and ability, we become prideful. This also can lead to our downfall. This faith walk is a journey, and there is always more to learn and discover. God brings us from faith to faith. When you become faithful in the little, He will give you more. Continue to seek His voice.

My experiences of traveling the world brought a fresh, new perspective to my life. It was so much more than just traveling; God opened up opportunities and strengthened muscles inside of me that I didn't even know existed. As I've continued to trust Him and allow Him to take control of my life, I've realized that His ways are so much better than mine. He really knows what's best for me. He created me. He has a plan and a purpose for me, and He does for you, too – just as he promises in Jeremiah 29:11:

"'For I know the plans I have for you,' declares the Lord, 'plans to prosper you and not to harm you, plans to give you a hope and a future.'"

He is faithful. Beware of the distractions. It's easy for us to be obedient for a short time, and then quit again. Being obedient to God can seem unpopular, difficult, painful, lonely, and unrewarding at times. Remember: Your life is your mission field, whether you are at the bank, driving in the car, or standing in a line waiting to pay. Let's let our lives reflect Whose we are and in Whom our hope is found.

When you are on the call or answer the call, don't overthink it. Remember it is by faith that we believe in God. It is by faith that we trust in Him and believe all His promises are true. Remember you are not alone, for there has been many before you. Even when do not understand, He always comes through. He will finish the good work He has started in you.

Hebrews 11: 3–35, which is the basis for the title of this book, states that it is:

*"**By faith** we understand that universe was formed at God's command, so that what is seen was not made out of what is visible.*

***By faith** Abel brought God a better offering than Cain did. By faith he was commanded as righteous, when God spoke well of his offerings. And by faith Abel still speaks, even though he is dead.*

***By faith** Enoch was taken from this life, so that he did not experience death: 'He could not be found, because God had taken him away.' For before he was taken, he was* commended as one who pleased God. And without faith it is impossible to please God, because anyone who comes to him must believe that he exists and that he rewards those who earnestly seek him.

By faith Noah, when warned about things not yet seen, in holy fear built an ark to save his family. By his faith he condemned the world and became heir of the righteousness that is in keeping with faith.

By faith Abraham, when called to go to a place he would later receive as his inheritance, obeyed and went, even though he did not know where he was going. By faith he made his home in the promised land like a stranger in a foreign country; he lived in tents, as did Isaac and Jacob, who were heirs with him of the same promise. For he was looking forward to the city with foundations, whose architect and builder is God.

And **by faith** even Sarah, who was past childbearing age, was enabled to bear children because she considered him faithful who had made the promise. And so from this one man, and he as good as dead, came descendants as numerous as the stars in the sky and as countless as the sand on the seashore.

All these people were still living by faith when they died. They did not receive the things promised: they only saw them and welcomed them from a distance, admitting that they were foreigners and strangers on earth. People who say such things show that they are looking for a country of their own. If *they had been thinking of the country they had left, they would have had opportunity to return. Instead, they were longing for a better country – a heavenly one. Therefore God is not ashamed to be called their God, for he has prepared a city for them.*

By faith Abraham, when God tested him, offered Isaac as a sacrifice. He who had embraced the promise was about to sacrifice his one and only son, even though God had said to him, "It is through Isaac that your offspring will be reckoned. Abraham reasoned that God could even raise the dead, and so in a manner of speaking he did receive Isaac back from the dead.

By faith Isaac blessed Jacob and Esau in regard to their future.

By faith Jacob, when he was dying, blessed each of Joseph's sons, and worshipped as he leaned on the top of his staff.

By faith Joseph, when his end was near, spoke about the exodus of the Israelites from Egypt and gave instructions concerning the burial of his bones.

By faith Moses' parents hid him for three months after he was born, because they saw be was no ordinary child, and they were not afraid of the king's edict.

By faith Moses, when he had grown up, refused to be known as the son of Pharaoh's daughter. He chose to be mistreated along with the people of God rather than to enjoy the fleeing pleasure of sin. He regarded disgrace for the sake of Christ as of greater value than the treasures of Egypt, because he was looking ahead to his reward. **By faith** *he left Egypt, not fearing the king's anger; he persevered because he saw him who is invisible.* **By faith** *he kept the Passover and the application of the blood, so that the destroyer of the firstborn would not touch the firstborn of Israel.*

By faith *the people passed through the Red Sea as on dry land; but when the Egyptians tried to do so, they were drowned.*

By faith *the walls of Jericho fell, after the army had marched around them for seven days.*

By faith *the prostitute Rahab, because she welcomed the spies, was not killed with those who were disobedient.*

And what more shall I say? I do not have time to tell about Gideon, Barak, Samson and Jephthah, about Daniel and Samuel and the prophets, who through faith conquered kingdoms, administered justice, and gained what was promised; who shut the mouths of lions, quenched the fury of the flames and escaped the edge of the sword; whose weakness was turned to strength; and who became powerful in battle and routed foreign armies. Women received back their dead, raised to life again."

"And I am certain that God, who began the good work within you, will continue his work until it is finally finished on the day when Christ Jesus returns." – Philippians 4:6 (NLT)

Resource Guide:

YOU CAN TRAVEL, TOO:
MISSION OPPORTUNITIES

If you have a heart to serve, then this section is for you! Many people have asked me what they can do for international missions, community outreach, and ministry opportunities or programs. I know what it is like to have a desire but not know exactly how to fulfill it, so I'm excited to share these with you! Below are more than 25 mission opportunities, in no particular order. I encourage you not only to research them, but also to seek God as you are thinking about them. Pray, and ask the Lord to direct your path. He will show you the steps to take. I'm excited for your journey!

The World Race

theworldrace.org

The World Race is an 11-month outreach program that takes participants to 11 different countries to minister to the poor, orphaned, and abandoned. They have multiple routes you can choose from that leave at different points throughout the year. I was first introduced to the World Race when I was an intern at Hillsong Church in South Africa. Members of the World Race would come and volunteer at many of our sites, as well as attend our services at church.

You are responsible for coming up with the costs of the trip. That fee includes flights, accommodation, and food. If you are interested in this, I would recommend checking out the blogs of recent and future racers. There is a page on The World Race website that provides links to the blogs of team members. Even if you are not interested in this trip, I would still recommend reading their blogs to hear their testimonies of God's provision for them during their race, how God changed their life, and how they were matured and stretched in the process. You will be encouraged!

Adventures in Missions
adventures.org

Adventures in Missions is the sister organization of The World Race. I first came to know of this organization from a friend who went on one of their mission trips to Thailand. Her life was radically changed. They have youth, college, short-term, long-term, and family mission trips to choose from. This is helpful in finding a trip to suit your needs, goals, and capacity. Service opportunities range from volunteering at human trafficking rescue organizations in Thailand to visiting orphanages in Africa. Check out their videos and visit their website to learn more!

Hillsong South Africa Internship
hillsong.co.za

If you have a heart to serve and love God, and if you don't mind living in one of the most beautiful cities on earth, then this internship might be right for you. This is what I did when I answered God's call to go to South Africa. It involves a year of Bible College studies and service within a department of church. Department opportunities include the Hillsong Africa Foundation (where I was placed), youth (includes services, raising up leaders, and outreach initiatives), worship, production team, creative team, and more! I'm sure there will be a department that will suit you and your strengths. This internship will grow your character and push you closer to God like never before. It is a year of growing and developing into your God-given potential. Success is not measured on how strong you develop a project, but on how you have grown and developed in your relationship with God. Visit the website to find out more!

Youth With A Mission (YWAM)
ywam.org

YWAM is the largest missions organization in the world. I've spoken to many people who have participated in one of their programs, and I've heard it described as 'a honeymoon with God.' YWAM has both long and short-term mission opportunities in more than 180 countries all over the world that you can choose from. They have outreach trips, discipleship training school, and other volunteer opportunities.

If you have a specific passion or hobby such as snowboarding, sailing, surfing, etc., you can find a training school or outreach program that will encourage and utilize your skills and interests. They have a variety of options, from spending six months doing outreach from a boat in the Asian Pacific to volunteering alongside organizations in Cambodia that are working to rescue human trafficking victims.

The best way to find out what any particular YWAM school

or location is about is to ask others who have been there. You could also visit YWAM's main Facebook page or the page of one of their specific locations. Contact their field locations directly to explore opportunities to serve. More information on how to contact them can be found on their website.

Iris Global
irisglobal.org

Iris Global has missions school in Mozambique, Brazil, and all over the world where they train you in the mission field, supernatural healings, and making disciples of all nations. To become a full-time missionary, you must first go through their Harvest School of Missions. They have both short-term and long-term mission schools. I know several people who have taken part in this ministry, and they were baptized in the Holy Spirit. It is a different element of faith.

Bethel School of Supernatural Ministry
bssm.net

This school based in Redding, California, teaches and equips you to become more in-tune with the Holy Spirit. For example, you go on treasure hunts where you pray, and God shows you people or things to look for. When you discover them, you pray for them on the spot. It is a prophetic school, and it's very inviting. I know of several people who have been to this school, and they loved it. There also is an optional mid-year missions trip.

Emirates Airlines: Cabin Crew

emiratesgroupcareers.com

In this position, you will be living in Dubai and traveling the world. Although this is not a "ministry" position, you will be a walking Bible. People will see how you respond in situations under pressure or in conflict, giving you an opportunity to be a light.

This position also will expose you to walks of life across the world, changing your perspective and mindset of what is truly out there. This could be the bridge that will lead you to the next place God has for you. The benefits include housing, transport and allowance in layover countries. It's an excellent job to help save money, as well as travel the world during your vacation times. I had more vacation days working there than in any other job. You can use those days to explore the world and see whatever your heart desires. It really is a once in a lifetime opportunity.

Hillsong Africa Foundation

hillsongafrica.com

This is a non-profit community outreach in Cape Town, South Africa, and it is the department of Hillsong Church I was placed in during my internship. You can volunteer for as little as a day or for a longer period of time. There are many amazing projects that you can get involved in, and you'll also have the chance to learn about the South African culture. You'll be led by and working with a world-class team. You'll grow in your relationship with God as you serve in the projects.

Hillsong Leadership College
hillsong.com/college

At this college based in Sydney, Australia, there are different streams you can study including pastoral leadership, worship, social justice, media, and more. I know several dozen people who have gone to this school, and they are seriously next-level in their leadership and walk with God. You don't necessarily have to be of "college" age to attend. There are people from their 30s to 50s that attend. You are never too old or to young. I highly recommend it!

International Missions Board
imb.org

Based in California, this program provides both short and long-term service opportunities. They also have a special program for Hispanic volunteers that allows them to maximize their unique cultural and linguistic skills when reaching areas on the mission field that other ethnicities may not in fulfilling the Great Commission.

Abolishing Injustice in the 21st Century (A21)
a21.org

This is a non-profit that believes we can end human trafficking together. It provides an amazing opportunity to volunteer in places all over the world and help end this modern day slavery. You can use skills such as marketing, communication, social media, journalism, administration, and more to help them in this mission. Locations to volunteer include Ukraine, United States, Australia, South Africa, Europe, and more.

Vision Rescue
visionrescue.co.in

Based in Mumbai, India, this non-profit empowers people to find their purpose, enjoy their rights, and live with dignity. Projects include work from providing education and nutrition to children on the streets of Mumbai to coming alongside the addicted population of Mumbai and helping them reclaim their lives.

Project Transformation
projecttransformation.org

This is program is based in the United States. If you have a passion for helping children improve their literacy skills and develop a love for reading, then this may be the perfect opportunity for you! They have several volunteer opportunities including after school, summer, and one-year programs.

Generation Transformation
umcmission.org

Based out of their head office in New York City, this program offers many young adult mission opportunities.

Volunteer options include two-year mission, two-month mission, and flexible mission service.

International House of Prayer (IHOP)
ihopkc.org

This Christian missions organization based in Kansas City, Missouri, focuses on prayer, worship, and evangelism.

Watoto
watoto.com

The Watoto model is designed to provide vulnerable women and children in Africa with holistic care and impact communities in the process. Opportunities include volunteering and helping the children and families in the communities for at least a month or more.

Amazima Ministries
amazima.org

Based in Uganda, this incredible ministry's projects involve relief work and development work, and they do it all while sharing the gospel of Jesus Christ at every turn in their journey. The founder of this organization has an incredible story, and their projects are worth supporting. Even if you can't afford to volunteer abroad, this program gives you the opportunity to sponsor a child.

Soul Church "Year of Your Life" Internship
soulchurch.com

This "Year of Your Life" program based in Norwich, England, gives you the opportunity to directly impact lives in Norwich and beyond. You'll be working with specific ministry departments, while also developing your own Godly character alongside existing church leaders.

Passion City Church "Intern Experience"
passioncitychurch.com

During this one-year internship based in Atlanta, Georgia, you will grow spiritually, personally, and professionally in profound ways, while also being developed as a leader.

Mercy Ships
mercyships.org

In this medical missions program, you'll travel by ship to the most vulnerable countries with lack of medical aid to heal the communities through surgeries that they do not have access to. You do not need to be a medical doctor to be a part of this mission. There are other opportunities on board that complete the full team that goes overseas!

UK – USA Ministries
uk-usaministries.com

Based in the United States, this organization partners with ministries in the UK, and they organize a program where you can serve for a year or more in the mission field. This includes serving God through ministering to young people, both in the local church and outside of it.

Loaves and Fishes International: Hidden Treasures

loavesandfishesintl.com

This is a foster home that cares for special needs children in China. The founders of this home have an incredible story. When they were living as a married couple in the United States, they stepped out in faith by resigning from their corporate jobs, selling their home and all of their belongings, and moving with their small children to start this foster home. All of this was on a word they received from God. This couple's story is also featured in the *Father of Lights* DVD that is included in this resource guide.

Charity Water Internship

charitywater.org

Based in New York City, this organization's mission is to bring clean and safe drinking water to every person in the world. Internship opportunities include strategy and business operations, accounting and finance, international expansion relationships, and so much more. The founder's story of how he started this organization is incredible and also worth researching.

Semester at Sea

semesteratsea.org

This program gives college students the opportunity to complete a semester aboard a ship that travels to different countries, explore and learn about different cultures, and gain hands-on experiences. In each country, you will have the opportunity to participate in field labs, field programs, and other activities that will help you push your understanding of the world in new directions.

Joyce Meyer, Hand of Hope

joycemeyer.org/handofhope

On outreach trips through this medical missions organization, you'll help save lives of those who otherwise may not have access to medical or dental care. Whether you're a dentist, family practitioner, chiropractor, medical assistant, phlebotomist, or licensed practical nurse, giving your time through one of their outreaches will be an experience you may never forget!

Peace Corps

peacecorps.gov

At this United States government-based organization, service opportunities involve immersing yourself in a community abroad and working side by side with their local leaders to tackle the most pressing challenges of our generation.

Volunteers come from all kinds of backgrounds. You can be just out of college, mid-career, or retired.

Compassion International
compassion.com

Use your talents and time on behalf of children in poverty around the world by volunteering through this incredible organization based in Colorado Springs. You can help make a difference one child at a time. Whether you volunteer at a Christian concert or festival or at Compassion headquarters, there are countless ways to make a difference!

Encouraging Tools:

Pinky Promise Movement

pinkypromisemovement.com

This is a community of women from all over the world that strive to honor God with their lives and bodies. They're not perfect, but they hold each other accountable and push each other closer to Christ through fellowship, fun outings, and monthly studies with one another. Find or start a group near you via their website!

Travel Noire

travelnoire.com

This is an amazing website that provides travel insight and connects others who have the interest of traveling! They even have meet-up groups where you can be inspired and learn the "ins and outs" of traveling in all seasons of life.

Secret Flying

secretflying.com

I love this website! They find amazing deals for flights to and from locations from all over the world. I recommend signing up for their newsletter to get instant notification of deals. They will notify you of the ones departing from your continent. This is great for when you go abroad on mission!

Music:

Praising God through worship music is another way to spend time with Him. Here are some songs on the playlist that I love to listen to when I need encouragement on my faith journey.

- "Trust" – Hillsong Young & Free
- "Desert Song" - Hillsong
- "Cornerstone" – Hillsong
- "Your Love Never Fails" – Jesus Culture
- "I Want to Know You" – Jesus Culture
- "Joy of the Lord (Live)" – Bethel Music and Jenn Johnson
- "Hosanna" – Hillsong
- "God is Able" - Hillsong
- "Healer" – Kari Jobe
- "God I Look to You" – Jenn Johnson (Bethel)
- "Never Alone" – Hillsong Young & Free
- "No Longer Slaves" - Steffany Frizzell-Gretzinger (Bethel Church)